Also by Carl Hiaasen
available from Random House Large Print

**Lucky You
Nature Girl**

The
Downhill
Lie

The Downhill Lie

A Hacker's Return to a Ruinous Sport

Carl Hiaasen

RANDOM HOUSE
LARGE PRINT

The Library of Congress Cataloging-in-Publication Data
Hiaasen, Carl.
The downhill lie : a hacker's return to a ruinous
sport / by Carl Hiaasen.—1st large print ed.
p. cm.
ISBN: 978-0-7393-2787-6 (lg. print)
1. Hiaasen, Carl. 2. Golfers—United States—
Biography. 3. Golf—United States.
4. Large type books. I. Title.
GV964.H43A3 2008
796.352092—dc22
[B]
2008008168

www.randomhouse.com/largeprint

FIRST LARGE PRINT EDITION

10 9 8 7 6 5 4 3 2 1

This Large Print edition published in accord with
the standards of the N.A.V.H.

"There is no comfort zone in golf."
—Tiger Woods

"If there's one thing golf demands
above all else, it's honesty."
—Jack Nicklaus

"When all is said and done, style is
function and function is style."
—Ben Hogan

"When you suck, you suck."
—Anonymous 16-handicapper

Preface

There are so many people to blame for this book that it's hard to know where to begin. At the top of the heap is my old buddy Joe Simmens, who got me golfing again for the first time since college. Next is Mike Lupica, who egged me on and conned me into keeping this journal, primarily for his own sick amusement.

At the Sandridge Golf Club I received deceptively promising lessons from Bob Komarinetz, an excellent instructor. Later I was inexplicably admitted to membership at the Quail Valley Golf Club, where Steve Mulvey, Kevin Given, Nate Tyler, Paul Grange, Jim Teed and many other good people declined to intervene and put an end to my misery.

It was at Quail Valley where two talented pros, Steve Archer and Mike Kotnik, spent long, valiant hours attempting to identify and repair my exotic swing flaws. The incomparable Delroy Smith caddied for many rounds, offering boundless encouragement even when it was patently futile.

My book editor, Peter Gethers, was no help at all. He insisted that I continue to write, no matter how rotten I was playing. In fact, the only person who offered to talk me out of this project was the notorious David Feherty of CBS Sports, but he's such a whack job that I didn't take him seriously.

Many friends willfully abetted my comeback by including me in their golf outings: Bill Becker, Paul Bogaards and all the crew from the class of '70 at Plantation High—"Big Al" Simmens, Jerry Miller, Tommy McDavitt, Steve Cascone, Larry Robinson, Mike Winchester and, last but not least, my tournament partner and unlicensed sports psychologist, Michael "Leibo" Leibick.

My own family cannot dodge some culpability for this misguided enterprise. My stepson, Ryan, helped pick out my first set of clubs; my wife, Fenia, bought me an elegant putter; my older son, Scott, never once tried to change my mind about doing this book, despite many opportunities; and my younger son, Quinn, has insisted on playing the game of golf with riotous mirth.

The person who first put a 5-iron in my hands all those years ago was my father, Odel Hiaasen. If he were still alive, this book would have turned out much differently—for one thing, he would have fixed my shanks by now.

Last on the list of conspirators is my loving mother, Patricia, who actually was pleased that I'd taken up golf again, and to this day believes it's been good for me.

I would never admit this, but she's been right before.

The
Downhill
Lie

Dawn of the Dead

In the summer of 2005, I returned to golf after a much needed layoff of thirty-two years.

Attempting a comeback in my fifties wouldn't have been so absurd if I'd been a decent player when I was young, but unfortunately that wasn't the case. At my best, I'd shown occasional flashes of competence. At my worst, I'd been a menace to all carbon-based life-forms on the golf course.

On the day I gave up golfing, I stood six-feet even, weighed a stringy 145 pounds and was in relatively sound physical shape. When I returned to the game, I was half an inch taller, twenty-one pounds heavier and nagged by the following age-related ailments:

The Downhill Lie

- elevated cholesterol;
- a bone spur deep in the right rotator cuff;
- an aching right hip;
- a permanently weakened right knee, due to a badly torn medial meniscus that was scraped and repaired in February 2003 by the same orthopedic surgeon who'd once worked on a young professional quarterback named Dan Marino. (The doctor had assured me that my injury was no worse than Marino's, then he'd added with a hearty chuckle, "But you're also not twenty-two years old.")

Other factors besides my knee joint and HDL had changed during my long absence. When I'd abandoned golf in 1973, I had been a happily married father of a two-year-old son. When I returned to the sport in 2005, I was a happily remarried father of a five-year-old son, a fourteen-year-old stepson and a thirty-four-year-old son with three kids of his own. In other words, I was a grandpa.

Over those three busy and productive decades, a normal, well-centered person would have mellowed in the loving glow of the family hearth. Not me. I was just as restless, consumed, unreflective, fatalistic and emotionally unequipped to play golf in my fifties as I was in my teens.

What possesses a man to return in midlife to a game at which he'd never excelled in his prime, and which in fact had dealt him mostly failure, angst and exasperation?

Here's why I did it: I'm one sick bastard.

The Last Waltz

My first taste of golf was as a shag caddy for my father. He often practiced hitting wedges in our front yard, and I'd put on my baseball glove and play outfield.

Dad seemed genuinely happy when I finally asked to take golf lessons. I was perhaps eleven or twelve, too young to realize that my disposition was ill-suited to a recreation that requires infinite patience and eternal optimism.

The club pro was Harold Perry, a pleasant fellow and a solid teacher. He said I had a natural swing, which, I've since learned, is what pros always say at your first lesson. It's more merciful than: "You'd have a brighter future chopping cane."

The early sessions did seem to go well, and Harold was encouraging. As time passed, however, he began chain-smoking heavily during our lessons, which suggested to me the existence of a chronic problem for which Harold had no solution. The problem was largely in my head, and fell under the clinical heading of Wildly Unrealistic Expectations.

My first major mistake was prematurely asking to join my father for nine holes, a brisk Sunday outing during which I unraveled like a crackhead at a Billy Graham crusade. This was because I'd foolishly expected to advance the golf ball down the fairway in a linear path.

The experience was marred by angry tears, muffled profanities and long, brittle periods of silence. Worse, a pattern was established that would continue throughout the years that Dad and I played together.

Golfers like maxims, and here's a good one: Beginners should never be paired with good players, especially if the good player is one's own father.

The harder I tried, the uglier it got. To say that I didn't bear my pain stoically is an understatement. Dad suffered along with me and so did his golf game, which added to my sullen mood an oppressive layer of guilt.

There were rare sunbursts of hope when I managed to hit a decent shot or sink a putt, but usually a pall of Nordic gloom followed us around the links. My father was a saint for tolerating my tantrums and sulking. He never once ditched me; whenever I asked to tag along on his regular weekend game, he'd say yes despite knowing what histrionics lay ahead. As I grew taller he generously bought me a set of Ben Hogans, which were so gorgeous that at first I was reluctant to throw them.

Interestingly, I have no recollection of my father and me completing a round of golf, with the exception of a father-son charity event (and the only reason I didn't flee on the back nine was that I wasn't sure how to get back to the clubhouse). I can't recall our final score, probably for the same reason that victims of serious traffic accidents often cannot remember getting in the car. Trauma wipes clean the memory banks.

In high school some of my friends took up golf, and occasionally I joined them on weekends. Surrounded by retirement developments, the Lauderdale Lakes course was a scraggly, unkempt layout that was chosen by us for its dirt-cheap, all-day green fees. Despite the trampled fairways and corrugated greens, I actually started enjoying myself—the mood was loose and raunchy, and it was uplifting to discover that my friends stroked the ball as erratically as I did. We were the youngest players on that course by half a century, a disparity that every round precipitated one or two prickly confrontations with foursomes who were less agile and alert. That, of course, only added to the sportive atmosphere.

Occasionally we also played a chaotic par-3 layout, upon which I once bladed a 9-iron dead into the cup for an ace. It was a feat that I never replicated. My name (misspelled, naturally) was etched into a hokey hole-in-one plaque that was hung among literally hundreds of others in the funky little clubhouse.

My father was undoubtedly relieved that I'd found other golfing companions, freeing him to resume his regular Sunday rounds in peace. Unfortunately, bursitis was making it increasingly difficult for him to swing a club, and by the time I left for college he was playing infrequently, and in pain.

During my first semester at Emory University I got married and soon thereafter became a father, so for a time I was too preoccupied—and too broke—for golf.

In the summer of 1972 I entered the journalism college at the University of Florida in

The Downhill Lie

Gainesville, where I reconnected with my high school buddies. The university maintains a top-notch par-72 that was in those days open to students for $2.50. It was there I broke 90 for the first and only time before giving up the game.

I was walking eighteen in a group that included a good friend, Al Simmens. He was hitting the ball well but I was all over the map, scrambling for bogeys and doubles. In the midst of butchering a long par-4, I improbably holed out a full 7-iron for a birdie. Exclamations of amused wonder arose from Big Al and the others. Then, supernaturally, two holes later I knocked in a 9-iron from about 110 yards.

This time Al keeled over as if felled by a sniper. Once before I'd seen him collapse like that on a golf course. It had happened when he was kneecapped by a drive struck by Larry Robinson, a member of our own foursome—the most astoundingly bad tee shot that I've ever witnessed, to this day. Al had been next up, standing dead even with Larry and seemingly safe, when Larry's abominably mishit ball shot off the tee at a 90 degree angle and smashed into Al's right leg. The impact sounded like a Willie McCovey home run. Incredibly, Al was upright within minutes, and resumed playing with only a slight limp.

But after my second hole-out on that morning in Gainesville, he lay lifeless in the fairway with a glassy expression that called to mind Queequeg, the Pacific Island cannibal in **Moby-Dick,** who'd lapsed into a grave trance upon seeing his fate in a throw of the bones. Eventually Al arose and rejoined our group, but he was rocky.

I completed the round with no further heroics yet I walked off the 18th green with an 88, my best score ever. That was in the summer of 1973, and by the end of the year I was done. The Hogans sat in a closet, gathering dust.

Richard Nixon was hunkered down like a meth-crazed badger in the White House,

The Downhill Lie

Hank Aaron was one dinger shy of Babe Ruth's all-time home run record, and The Who had just released **Quadrophenia**.

At age twenty, I was more or less at peace.

Toad Golf

My divorce from golf was uncomplicated and amicable. When I came home from college on visits, my father and I would spend Sunday afternoons watching the PGA on television. Dad had always asserted that Sam Snead was the greatest player of all time, but he was gradually coming around to the possibility that Jack Nicklaus was something special.

Then, in February 1976, my father died suddenly at the outrageously unfair age of fifty, a tragedy that extinguished any lingering whim I might have had to tackle golf again with serious intent. Apparently I played a round later that year with a friend, although my memory of it is fogged.

Possibly I've blocked out other rounds, too. My brother, Rob, says that he and I golfed together one time not long after Dad passed away. "It wasn't good," he tells me.

The next time I recall swinging a club wasn't in any conventional, or socially acceptable, format.

It occurred one night that same year, when my best friend and fishing companion, Bob Branham, called to report a disturbing infestation. The culprit was **Bufo marinus**, a large and brazen type of toad that had invaded South Florida from Central America and proliferated rapidly, all but exterminating the more docile native species. The **Bufo** grows to two pounds and eats anything that fits in its maw, including small birds and mice. When threatened, it excretes from two glands behind its eyes a milky toxin extremely dangerous to mammals. Adventuresome human substance abusers have claimed that licking **Bufo** toads produces psychedelic visions, but the practice is often fatal for dogs and cats.

Which is why Bob had called. Every evening a brigade of **Bufo**s had been appearing outside his back door and gobbling all the food he'd put out for Dixie, his young Labrador retriever. It's probably unnecessary to point out that while Labradors possess a cheery and endearing temperament, they are not Mensa candidates in the kingdom of canines. In fact, Labs will eagerly eat, lick or gnaw objects far more disgusting than a sweaty toad. For that reason, Bob expressed what I felt was a well-founded fear that his beloved pet was in peril during these nightly **Bufo** encounters.

When I arrived at his house, the onslaught was in progress. A herd of medium-sized toads hungrily patrolled the perimeter of his patio, while one exceptionally rotund specimen had vaulted into Dixie's dish and engulfed so much dog chow that it was unable to climb out. It looked like a mud quiche with eyeballs.

As kids, Bob and I had roamed the Everglades collecting wild critters, so neither of us wanted to harm the **Bufo**s. Yet there seemed no choice but to remove them quickly and by force, before his dopey dog slurped one like a Popsicle.

Ballasted with Alpo, the toads would have been easy to capture by hand. That, however, would have presented two serious problems. One was the poison; the other was pee. Toads are prodigious pissers, and **Bufo**s in particular own hair-trigger bladders. The instant you pick one up, the hosing commences and does not cease until you drop it.

Bob and I were discussing our limited and unsavory options when I noticed a golf bag in a corner near the back door. We had a brief conversation about which of his neighbors was the most obnoxious, and then I reached for a 9-iron. Bob chose a 7.

Before the PETA rally begins, let me point out that an adult **Bufo** toad is one of God's sturdiest creatures. Bob swears he once saw one get run over by a compact car and then hop away. I have my doubts, but in any case we purposely picked lofted clubs to effect a kinder, gentler relocation.

The Downhill Lie

Aerodynamically, your average toad travels through the air with substantially more drag than a golf ball. This is because golf balls are usually round, and legless. A toad won't carry as far, or roll more than once or twice when it lands. Nonetheless, I soon found the range with Bob's 9-iron, chipping several beefy **Bufo**s onto a window awning two houses away. Even at that distance we could hear the feisty invaders clomping across the flimsy aluminum before free-falling into the backyard of their new, unsuspecting hosts.

Purists probably wouldn't consider clandestine toad launching as true golf, but for accuracy's sake it must be reported that I took five or six swings with an iron that night. The next time I touched a club was in August 1977, while vacationing in Asheville, North Carolina. The trip stands out for two reasons: Elvis Presley died that week, and I got my first (and last) taste of genuine mountain moonshine. However, I was neither grief-stricken nor bombed when I accompanied a friend to a municipal

driving range, which—using borrowed clubs—
I chopped into wet clots of flying sod.

During self-imposed retirement I continued
to follow the professional tour as a fan, and in
1978 I even attended what was then called the
Jackie Gleason Inverrary Classic in Lauderhill.
On the afternoon that I was in the gallery, Nicklaus ran off five consecutive birdies on his way to
dusting the field. His performance was so other-
wordly that it validated my decision to abandon
the game; the only way I belonged on a golf
course was as a spectator.

Then, in November 2002, another slip
occurred, and it ultimately set me on the cart
path to perdition.

Monkey Golf

The trouble began when Terry McDonell of
Sports Illustrated asked me to write a

The Downhill Lie

humorous piece of fiction for the magazine's hugely popular swimsuit issue. The "research" would involve traveling to Barbados to observe a photo shoot featuring exotic supermodels in microscopic bikinis.

I told Terry I'd have to think about it, a hesitancy he did not often encounter when offering swimsuit-issue assignments. However, I needed time to compose a description of the project that would sound reasonable to my beautiful Greek wife, deft as she is with cutlery.

For not the first time, imagination failed me—there was no way to put "Barbados" and "supermodels" in the same sentence and sell the trip as anything but a spectacular boondoggle, a Caribbean fantasy camp for aging males.

"Bring Fenia along," Terry suggested.

"Done."

The magazine put us up at a well-known and preposterously expensive resort called Sandy Lane, which would later become more famous as the place where Tiger Woods got married.

My editor, Bob Roe, arrived hauling a set of golf clubs. Having journeyed to many tropical locations for previous swimsuit editions, Roe was not breathlessly fascinated with the proceedings. The only golfer in the magazine's entourage, he'd disappear each afternoon to play one of the rambling eighteen-hole layouts at Sandy Lane.

Meanwhile I was dutifully monitoring the photo sessions on the beach, taking notes and—dare I admit?—getting bored.

You're thinking: How is that possible? **Sports Illustrated**'s models are the most breathtaking women in the world!

The point cannot be argued. However, fashion shoots can be as sappingly tedious as moviemaking. There were long and frequent delays for weather, lighting, makeup, hair styling, thong alterations and even crowd control. My mission was not to chronicle the scene as a journalist but rather to troll for potentially satiric material. After a couple of days, I'd collected more than enough.

One evening at dinner, Roe and I started chatting about golf. Foolishly I mentioned that I'd played when I was young.

The Downhill Lie

"Why don't you come out with me tomorrow? It'll be fun," he said.

"No, thanks."

"They've got monkeys out there," he added matter-of-factly.

"What kind of monkeys?"

Roe shrugged. "How should I know?"

I was aware that golf had changed during my three-decade abstinence, but I had no idea that prestigious courses were now being stocked with wild, free-ranging primates. Who in their right mind could pass up a day of monkey golf?

The following afternoon, Roe and I set out for Sandy Lane's Country Club course, designed by the renowned golf architect Tom Fazio. Roe assured me that the shareholders of Time Warner would be delighted to rent me a set of clubs and pay my green fees. They even kicked in for a golf glove and a sleeve of balls.

Waiting on the first tee, I was no more anxious than a cliff diver in a hurricane. My rented driver bore little resemblance to the old persimmons I'd used as a kid—the club-head was as large as Ozzy Osbourne's liver, and made of a distractingly shiny alloy. I have no memory of that first shot, though I feel confident to report that it did not sail 260 yards down the center of the fairway.

Fortunately, Roe is a witty, easygoing guy, and after a few holes my nerves began to settle. For not having played in so long, I was striking the ball shockingly well. I still couldn't putt worth a damn, but I finished the front nine only 10-over-par, a respectable number considering my extended layoff.

On the back side, those eons without practice caught up. My swing disintegrated and so did my score. I began to notice that whenever I approached my ball, Roe, who stands about six-feet-five, would discreetly endeavor to align himself behind a coconut palm, or cower in a vale of dense shrubbery. At one point, our mild-mannered caddy snatched the 3-wood from my hand and declared that I was no longer allowed to touch it.

Frankly, I wasn't as dismayed by my rusty

play as I was by the lack of marauding primates, and I raised with Roe the issue of false advertising. If a golf course promises monkeys, then, by God, there ought to be monkeys.

The caddy expressed authentic surprise that we hadn't encountered any of the beasts, which he described as fearless and coarse. The only species found on Barbados is an Old World vervet, the African green monkey, which arrived more than three centuries ago with slave traders from Senegal and Gambia. Today the island's simian population is estimated at five thousand to seven thousand individuals, a somewhat speculative figure given the logistical challenges of monkey census taking.

African greenies aren't large—adult males grow only sixteen inches tall, and a ten-pounder would be considered a cruiserweight. But because they sometimes roam in hordes, the possibility for mayhem is omnipresent. I tried to remain upbeat while hacking my way through the last nine.

Finally, as Roe and I stood beneath a tree

on the 13th tee, something rustled heavily in the branches above us.

"There's one!" the caddy cried, with a ring of vindication.

We looked up just in time to see a tawny form darting among the limbs, but just as swiftly it disappeared. In vain we waited for a display of monkey hijinks, but all remained quiet at the top of the tree. The caddy insisted that what we'd seen was an African green, and I politely pretended to believe him. In truth I suspected it was a large squirrel, or even a feral cat.

Roe and I teed off without incident. Heading down the fairway, I watched for movement in the foliage. If a troop of monkeys was tailing us, they were uncharacteristically stealthy and well disciplined.

Roe hit a terrific second shot that landed four feet from the pin. I took my usual ping-pong route to the hole, putted out and stepped away while he lined up a birdie attempt.

As he steadied himself over the ball, I happened to glance back down the fairway—and there, loping boldly toward us with its tail erect, was a robust, full-grown **Chlorocebus aethiops.**

Since that day, I've apologized numerous times to Roe for what happened next. Indefensibly, inexcusably, I got carried away by the unfolding scene, a genuine Animal Planet moment.

At the precise instant that Roe drew back his putter, I excitedly blurted out: "Look at that fucking monkey!"

Two things happened next, both predictable: The monkey ran away, and Bob missed the putt.

A golfing tradition that hadn't changed during my absence was the strict code of etiquette. When a player is putting, his companions are expected to remain still and be silent. My untimely outburst might have been forgivable if the monkey had presented a clear and present danger—say, if it was drooling with rabies, or armed with a sharp stick.

It wasn't. The animal was simply bounding toward the green, probably to beg for a snack.

I felt so badly about Roe missing his birdie that I urged him to try the putt again. He did.

And pulled it to the left, the same as before.

"Do it over," I implored. "This is all my fault."

He told me not to worry about it, and tapped in for his par. He remained so good-natured about the fiasco that I was crippled with guilt for several holes. Thank God no other monkeys showed up.

The 18th was a downhill par-3 to the clubhouse. I could see tourists sipping cocktails on the broad veranda and looking out toward the green. A bitter knot gathered in my stomach. It seemed only fitting that I should finish the day as comic relief, considering my **faux paw,** as it were, on the 13th.

Yet, against all odds, I stuck a 6-iron

about thirty feet from the hole and two-putted for par.

It was the worst possible thing that could have happened, because I walked off that course believing I could actually play this damn game again.

One day.

Maybe.

If I put some work into it . . .

The following morning, Roe asked if I wanted to try another round. I almost said yes, but then I remembered how golf goes: One day you're suckered into self-confidence by making a few decent shots; the next day you can't hit the green with a sledgehammer, and your spirit is crushed like an insect.

So I politely declined the invitation, and spent the remainder of the trip on the beach with my wife and little boy, watching half-naked supermodels pose for pictures.

Foolishly I brought home a pink Sandy Lane golf tee as a souvenir of the **Sports Illustrated** gig. I should have thrown the stupid thing away, but instead I placed it on a bookshelf in my office, in plain view, a constant reminder of that sunny day in Barbados.

What the hell was I thinking?

Total Relapse

Golf books are laced with aphorisms and pithy one-line nuggets of advice because golfers aren't supposed to overload their brains. "Swing thoughts" should be few and simple, according to the experts. One's mind should be uncluttered, and at ease.

Unfortunately, the single most important fact about golf is as calming as a digital prostate exam: It's hard.

Ridiculously hard, if your goal is to play well.

When I decided to reconnect with the game, I had no illusions about getting really good at it. I just wanted to be better at **something** in middle age than I was when I was young.

The golf industry estimates that between

two million and three million newcomers take up the sport every year, but there is no reliable statistic on recidivists like me.

For many of those golf-free years I'd lived down in the Florida Keys, where I pursued a passion for fly-fishing. My preferred quarry was bonefish, a swift and skittish species that must be stalked while wading, or poling a flat-bottom skiff across the shallows. Bonefish are often difficult to find, and even more difficult to fool with a pinch of rooster feathers tied on a bare hook. They are among the fastest fish in the sea but, being neither tasty nor impressively large, their appeal is limited to anglers of an intense and arcane bent.

In the summer of 2005, our family moved up the coast to Vero Beach, where there are no bonefish to be caught. Consequently I found myself lacking an unhealthy obsession, a perilous state for a writer.

As it happened, the contractor building our new house was Joe Simmens, the older brother of Big Al, my high school classmate and former golfing companion. Joe had a summer membership at one of the local clubs, and he asked if I wanted to join him for nine holes one afternoon.

No thanks, I said.

Joe kept after me, and to this day I truly believe that he meant no harm; he was just trying to be friendly.

Eventually, I caved. We played a quick nine and it wasn't a total disaster; in fact, it was pleasant. I had a few good holes, which is all that any dumbass needs to fool himself into thinking he's got talent.

Days later, Joe and I played again. There were fewer bright moments, and less cause for hope, but I managed to convince myself that I was struggling because I was using borrowed clubs.

So I took the next step: I went shopping for my own sticks.

What triggered such an impulsive and chancy decision is hard to say. Time, lurking like a starved jackal, was surely a factor. If I ever were to try golf again, the battle had to be joined while I was still ambulating with pin-free joints and uncompressed vertebrae.

It would be the beginning, I knew, of a weird and self-pulverizing journey. Like a true masochist, I kept notes.

Day 1

My teenaged stepson, Ryan, agrees to accompany me to a store that specializes in secondhand golf equipment. Everywhere I look are gleaming clusters of pre-owned, metal-head drivers. After a few minutes of puzzled meandering, I confess to Ryan that I have no idea what kind of clubs to buy.

Finally, while browsing through the bags, I spot a familiar and hallowed name: Nicklaus.

I snatch up the set and approach the register, where an amused-looking salesman assures me that the clubs will fit just fine. The previous owner, he says, was exactly

my height and build. I hand over my
credit card.

Ryan asks, "What about a glove?"

"Oh yeah. I'll take a glove, too."

"And don't forget some balls," Ryan says.

"Right. Good idea."

The total bill: $164.21. Some guys
spend more than that on a putter.

My plan, though, is to start cheap.
Minimizing the investment in golf gear
should make it easier not to take the game
so seriously and, if necessary, allow for an
honorable retreat. Dropping fifteen
hundred bucks on a new set of clubs
would have been a heavy, long-term
commitment—who needs that kind of
pressure?

Pleased with my strategy, I walk out of
the store toting an almost pristine set of
Golden Bear TranZitions with a "light
reflex" .370 tip, reinforced with titanium. I
have no clue what any of that means, but
I'm about to find out.

Lesson One

Indian River County has good public golf courses, including Sandridge, where I started hitting once or twice a week on the practice range. No two shots followed the same trajectory; every swing was high drama.

Before long, I screwed up the courage to schedule a lesson with the club pro, Bob Komarinetz, an outgoing fellow and also an avid fisherman. He watched me hit about a dozen balls, then politely inquired about my clubs. I handed him the TranZition driver, which he examined somewhat skeptically.

"It's too short for you," he said, "and too light."

The shaft, he added, was whippy. "The clubhead turns at impact, because of the torque," he explained. "That's what's causing your slice."

"What about my hook?"

Komarinetz cleared his throat.

"And my shank?" I said.

"You should learn on clubs that fit you. These are okay for now, but if you change your mind I can loan you some others."

I hit some more shots. Every once in a while, one of them would go straight.

"The guy who sold me the set said the original owner was the same height as I am," I offered lamely.

Komarinetz looked doubtful. "The clubs would work fine for an older person," he said, "someone with a much slower swing."

"In other words, the last person who used these was probably in his what—seventies or eighties?"

Komarinetz saw that I was bummed about getting suckered at the golf store. Like any good teacher, he wanted to buoy my spirits.

"Let me see you hit a few 5-irons," he suggested.

From then on it wasn't easy to concentrate, knowing that my clubs were better fitted for Mickey Rooney.

Still, I swung away stubbornly and vowed

to stick with my plan. As long as I was carrying secondhand sticks, I could quit the game all over again anytime I wanted, with no harm done. At worst, I'd be out $164 and a little bit of pride.

So I resolved to grind it out with my geriatric Golden Bears.

Day 30

I play nine holes, and I don't hit a single drive that flies more than a few feet off the ground. It's a good thing there are no gophers in Florida because I would've killed a bunch. By the end of the afternoon, I'm praying for double-bogeys.

And, of course, hating my clubs.

Day 41

So much for my grand plan; I've got no chance with these TranZitions. It's like hitting with chopsticks.

Komarinetz loans me a set of adult-sized

Callaways, and I shoot 48 on the front nine, including two pars. I blow up on a couple of holes but overall it's not too awful.

The next step is to ditch the Golden Bears.

Sorry, Jack.

Loyalty is fine, but pain is pain.

Outside Agitators

Before recommitting to golf, I consulted with several friends, most of whom expressed surprise and a certain twisted glee. One was Mike Leibick, a marvelously sardonic character with whom I attended high school and college. Over the last thirty years Leibo has developed into an appallingly good golfer. Now a vice president of Bacardi, his travels take him to some of the most hallowed golf shrines in the country, from Pebble Peach to Pinehurst.

The Downhill Lie

A naturally gregarious fellow, Leibo is equally at ease among strangers and friends. I am the polar opposite.

What had drawn me to bonefishing was the solitary and natural setting—poling the tropical shallows alone, or with a guide, in a small skiff. It's a peaceful but focused state of isolation that I was hoping to replicate on the golf course.

"I just want to be able to sneak out after work and play nine holes all by myself," I told Leibo. "You've gotta understand: There are only a few people in the world I can stand to be around."

"You've got to get over that," he said.

"Why? I go fishing alone all the time."

"But golf is a **social** sport."

"Hey, I'll mind my own business. I won't cause any trouble."

"This oughta be good," he said.

The first time I got up the nerve to play with Leibo, I parred the opening hole. He tried not to appear shocked.

"Just wait," I told him, and promptly I triple-bogeyed the second.

"Ray-Ray golf," Leibo explained with a grim nod.

"Which is?"

"One hole you play like Ray Floyd, and the next you play like Ray Charles."

"That's me!" I said. "I'm the poster child."

Another person in whom I confided was Mike Lupica, the popular novelist and ace sports columnist for the New York **Daily News.**

"Are you sure you want to do this?" he asked when I told him I'd bought some secondhand clubs.

"I've got to do **something** or I'm gonna drive Fenia crazy," I said.

Lupica started playing golf at the same young age as I did, but he didn't pause to take thirty years off. Consequently, he now owns a single-digit handicap and hits the ball straight as a dream.

While he has been outwardly sympathetic to my tribulations on the golf course, he freely admits to having many laughs at my expense. It was Lupica, abetted by the great Pete Hamill, who suggested that I start keeping a golf diary. And it was Lupica who, whenever I threatened to quit the sport again, talked me down off the ledge.

Once I felt the need to apologize for a hail of self-flagellating e-mails.

"I'll stop whining," I promised.

"Are you insane?" Lupica shot back. "Whining is one of the rock-solid foundations of golf."

That's all I needed to hear.

Day 57

E-mail to Leibo: "What's the record for the number of golf balls lost in nine holes? And why doesn't someone invent a tee that you can slit your wrists with?"

Day 59

"Golf free the rest of your life!"

This is the sales pitch of a mammoth retirement development called The Villages, located south of Ocala in what

was once the tranquil horse country of
Florida. Commercials for The Villages
run frequently during televised PGA events
and also on the Golf Channel, which,
disturbingly, I've begun watching late at
night if Letterman is a rerun. The ads show
"active" seniors dancing, playing softball
and, most festively, marching the links.

Only briefly do I try to imagine what it
would be like to spend my final days on
earth among 100,000 aging but feisty golf
fanatics. Where in Dante's elaborate
infrastructure of Hell would such a place fit?

The Villages is so enormous that it sprawls
across three counties, and has its own
development district. The favorite mode of
transportation is the private golf cart, and a
special driver-safety course is available for
inexperienced newcomers. Among the
diversions are two fitness centers, a wood
shop, a polo field, an archery range, two
libraries and thirty recreation complexes,
most with heated swimming pools.

Golf, though, is the foremost attraction;

golf, golf and more golf. The development offers a boggling choice of twenty-eight courses, eight of which are full-length championship tracts. The rest are short executive layouts and, not surprisingly, the only ones that residents may play free forever.

The Villages surely is the place to be if your dream is to drop dead in your FootJoys. The youngest age allowed is fifty-five, so in less than two years I'll be eligible to move in and tee up with the other grandpas, if my wife dumps me in the interim. Should my relationship with golf turn sour, I could always take up ashtray carving, the long bow or possibly the breaststroke.

Or I could just hang myself and get it over with.

Day 60

Piled up a 103 at Sandridge, just dreadful. I'm breaking down and ordering those Callaways tomorrow.

As if it'll make a difference.

Emotional Rescue

Golf was supposed to be easier the second time around.

That's what everybody told me. Because of the amazing new high-tech equipment, they said, your drives will launch higher and farther, your irons will fly straighter, your putts will roll truer.

It was a lovely world to hope for, but I remained wary. One thing I remembered too clearly from the old days: No matter what club was in my hands, a bad swing invariably produced a bad result.

The revolution in golf technology that occurred during my long sabbatical was driven by two corollary, and ultimately successful, missions. The first was to expand the popularity of the sport by convincing millions of nongolfers that, with properly tuned and fitted weapons, the game really wasn't so difficult to conquer.

The Downhill Lie

A second and equally lucrative target was those souls who already played the game but did so in a mode of perpetual discouragement, approximately 98 percent of the USGA membership. The industry correctly calculated that vast fortunes could be reaped if the average player could be persuaded that his or her score would be instantly improved by purchasing an expensive new set of sticks, a ritual ideally repeated every two or three years.

To shield the touchy egos of hackers, golf manufacturers perfected a lexicon of gentle euphemisms. "Forgiving" is now the favored buzzword used to promote clubs designed for the Neanderthal swing. "Tour models" are for good players, "game-improvement" selections are for weekend warriors, and the "**maximum game-improvement**" aisle is reserved for the congenitally hapless.

When researching which clubs would be best for a middle-aged recidivist nursing a banged-up knee, I was overwhelmed by the multitude of choices—and baffled by the specifications.

An advanced degree from MIT would have helped when I went shopping for a driver. The loft angles varied from 7.5 degrees to 15 degrees, and one particular Mizuno was available in twenty-nine different shafts. The innards of Ping's G5 were supposedly computer-engineered with a process called "finite-element analysis," a term that for all I know was stolen from an old **Star Trek** episode.

The promotional literature abounded with confusing references to "MOI," or moment of inertia, which describes a clubhead's tendency to twist when it strikes the ball. The greater the measured MOI, the more stable the clubface remains at impact, theoretically producing a straighter, longer shot.

Several brands of drivers allow players to experiment with the MOI by manually rearranging imbedded weights. The 460cc Cleveland Launcher touts a "beta-titanium insert" that is "robotically plasma-welded to expand the sweet spot." Meanwhile Taylor-Made heavily advertises a SuperQuad edition with "four movable weight screws" that may be adjusted to six different centers of gravity. Unfortunately, the $400 purchase price doesn't include a Black & Decker drill kit.

The last thing I wanted was a driver that came with an instruction manual. I can't assemble a toy train track without leaving blood on the floor, so I wasn't about to tinker with high-priced golfing equipment. The only "moment of inertia" that affects me is the one that occurs every time I stand over the ball, frozen with trepidation.

Friends said that choosing that first set of modern clubs would be a midlife-altering experience, and they encouraged me to consult a professional fitter who could determine the head weights, shafts, lengths and lofts appropriate for my swing.

The problem was, I didn't have one swing; I had many.

Every time I went to the practice range I was a different golfer—a male Sybil in spikes. (Speaking of which, FootJoy is now marketing a golf shoe with plastic knobs on the heels, for personalized adjusting in case your toes suddenly swell up in the middle of a round.)

Being inconsistently inconsistent, I was a club fitter's nightmare. A driver, for example, was in my hands an instrument of infinite possibilities. Five consecutive swings might produce (and I've kept track): a monster slice, a snap hook, a push, a pull and a wormburner. There's no single technological solution to such random dysfunction.

So I decided to go basic, ordering a full set of Callaway Big Berthas recommended by Bob Komarinetz at Sandridge. Having given me some lessons, he was familiar with my array of unpredictable though innovative swing flaws.

The Callaways were straight from the catalogue, the only modification being half-inch-longer shafts for the irons. The first time I used them wasn't exactly an epiphany, since I had played with graphite loaners, but I hit enough decent shots to realize that I'd have no excuse for not improving.

The Downhill Lie

In their appearance, feel and impact, the new lightweight clubs bore no comparison to what I remembered of my uncompromising old Hogans. The most startling difference was the length off the tee—I'd never knocked a golf ball that far when I was younger.

There's a good reason why equipment companies hype distance more than any other feature; nothing inflates the vanity of a male hacker as much as bombing a huge drive. And no other facet of the sport has changed so radically since its beginnings. **Golf Magazine** recently asked a 6-handicapper to hit some Titleist Pro V1s with a new 460cc driver and a hickory-shafted model of the sort used a century ago. The average carry of the titanium driver was 220 yards, compared to 179 yards with the wooden club. When the test golfer switched to an old-style gutta-percha ball—a one-piece ball packed internally with dried gum—the modern driver outdistanced the antique even farther, 205 yards to 126 yards.

Most pros adore the new juiced balls and melon-shaped metalwoods, too. Today the average drive on the PGA tour goes 283 yards, compared to 255 yards back in 1968. While the hot new technology favors big hitters, the holes have become shorter for everyone. Consequently, many older courses have been redesigned to create more difficulties for the musclebound, and almost all the newer courses are longer and less hospitable to bombers.

As pleased as I was about the robust tee shots, I had no illusions that my game would be miraculously elevated. The extra length was meaningless—and sometimes catastrophic—if the ball was traveling on an errant line, which was a frequent problem.

Even hitting it straight didn't guarantee more pars and birdies. A driver comes out of the bag only fourteen times per round, at the most. Lots of players can bang it plenty far but can't score because they're helpless with their irons, wedges and putter. That would be me.

My most productive experiment with twenty-first-century golf weaponry resulted from a round with Mike Leibick, soon after I'd started playing again. On the first hole, with his ball lying 170 yards from the stick, he unsheathed a club unlike anything I'd ever seen. Its shiny teardrop head resembled a dwarf fairway metal or possibly a pregnant putter, fixed on a stout graphite shaft.

"What is **that**?" I asked.

"A rescue club."

"You're kidding."

"You definitely need to get yourself one of these," Leibo said, and knocked the shot pin-high.

Also known as hybrids or utility clubs, they were first developed to replace long irons, which many average golfers find difficult to hit well consistently. Leibo, a very good player, told me that switching to hybrids had saved his fairway game.

"There's a reason they're called rescue clubs," he said. "Anybody can hit one of these things. It's impossible **not** to."

My set of Callaways didn't include a 3-iron, so—after asking around—I filled the gap with a two-toned 22 degree Cleveland Halo. As odd as it looked, the hybrid performed surprisingly well, and not just from the tight cut.

Because the heads of so-called utility models are smooth and roundish, they don't grab or dig on mishits like a conventional blade can. That's one reason that hybrids are much easier to launch from the rough, and even from fairway bunkers. Another nifty design feature is the exaggerated "face-to-back dimension," which positions the center of gravity farther from the point of impact, generating a higher ball flight.

I was grateful to Leibo for introducing me to the wonders of rescue clubs, but he was dead wrong about one thing: It's **not** impossible to hit them badly. Along with some very presentable shots, I've unleashed some memorable stinkers—corkscrews, pop flies, wounded jackrabbits; flight patterns that the best technicians at Cleveland Golf could never reproduce on a simulator.

This is another immutable truth about the sport: The equipment can't save you from yourself. On a good day, a good golfer will shoot lights-out using any set of clubs. On a bad day, a bad golfer will butcher the easiest course in the county with $2,000 worth of plasma-welded hardware in his bag.

An old friend, Dan Goodgame, carries the same persimmon woods and bone-jarring Hogan blades that he was using more than thirty years ago, when we last teed off together—and he still plays well. Conversely, the golf club has not been invented that I can't find a way to disgrace.

A hybrid might rescue a player from a bad lie, but there is no rescue from a bad swing. When you suck, you suck.

Day 98

I phone my wife to tell her that I birdied one of those nasty par-3s that always gives me fits. She congratulates me enthusiastically, but later confesses that she has no idea what a birdie is.

Day 102

From an e-mail to Leibo:

"I shot a 49 at Sandridge but I didn't have any three-putts. How the fuck is that possible? Lost not one but two balls on a par-5, and got a 9 on the hole."

Leibo responds: "I have a solution. Don't play the par-5s."

He might be serious.

Day 113

As a surprise, my wife buys me a 35-inch Scotty Cameron American Classic, a milled flange that looks like a work of modern art.

Even if the occasion calls for it, I'll never have the heart to wrap this lovely putter around a pine tree.

Gimme Shelter

For the solitary, anxiety-ridden golfer, public links are slow torture. One solution is to have your own backyard golf course. In Bridgehampton, New York, somebody is selling a sixty-acre retreat with a twenty-thousand-square-foot mansion, fourteen gardens and a nine-hole layout complete with a pro shop. Price: $75 million.

A less extravagant option is to join a country club, then sneak out to play in off-hours or foul weather, when the course is nearly deserted.

The summer and early fall are prime in Florida, because that's when the heat becomes so suffocating that most club players flee north. Those who remain venture out while the morning dew is still on the grass, and hurry to complete their rounds before the sun gets high. By mid-afternoon, most private courses are as barren as the bleachers at a Marlins game.

Soon after we moved to Vero Beach, my wife learned of a club called Quail Valley, which offers tennis, yoga, a fitness center, two good restaurants and a large swimming pool for the kids. It also features a golf course designed by Nick Price and Tom Fazio, which guarantees a degree of difficulty far beyond what's advisable for an aging second-timer. The regulars call it "Gale Valley," which, I would soon discover, was not hyperbole.

The course was carved from a flat 280-acre orange grove, sculpted with two million cubic yards of fill and elevated to heights of forty feet. The dirt was excavated on site, the ensuing craters converted to a daunting network of ball-eating lakes, ponds and sloughs.

Bill Becker, a friend and a first-rate player, gave me a tour of the layout on a breezy December day. I hadn't seen so much water since Hurricane Donna swamped the state in 1960.

The Downhill Lie

Noticing the dread in my eyes, Bill tried to calm me. "The fairways are actually pretty wide," he kept saying.

Yet all I could think was: I must be out of my frigging mind.

From the blue tees at Quail, the USGA Course Rating is 71.4 and the Slope is 133. Not a cakewalk.

Still, the place was pretty and, more importantly, quiet. Bill promised I'd be able to play a quick and solo nine holes practically any afternoon, even during the winter season. It was an enticing pitch.

Later we visited the clubhouse, where taxidermied heads of elk, moose and other deceased ungulates gazed down from the walls. Upon entering the men's locker area, I was startled to see a stuffed African lion, as well as an upright brown bear, its face locked in a somewhat befuddled snarl. Bill assured me that the mounts were only decorative, and that bagging large game was not a requirement for membership.

I liked that Quail Valley was freestanding

and wide open, not pinched inside a residential development. Its rural, agriculturally zoned site had been selected specifically to minimize the possibility—or at least forestall the day—that it will be surrounded by houses and condos, a depressingly common fate.

In Florida it's rare to find a new golf course that was built purely for the experience of the sport. Most courses are conceived as the centerpiece excuse for some mammoth high-end real-estate project, the mission being to wring every last dime of profit from every square foot.

Not far from Naples is an 868-acre "community" called West Bay, supposedly "dedicated to preserving the surrounding environment." Indeed, developers have set aside about five hundred acres of woods and wetlands, and built an ecologically copacetic golf tract that earned a coveted "sanctuary" designation from Audubon International.

Yet within this setting are no fewer than eight subdivisions offering single-family houses, estate homes and compact crossbreeds called "carriage homes," meaning they are small enough to be pulled by horses. None of the units are cheap, and the developers have gotten rich.

But not rich enough, as they're now topping off two twenty-story towers on the shore of Estero Bay—just an elevator ride and a short stroll to the first tee.

I take the old-fashioned position that golf was not meant to be played in the shadow of a high-rise; that high-rises don't belong on the banks of an estuary; and that whoever is responsible for such abominations should be pounded to a permanently infertile condition with a 60-degree lob wedge.

Some golfers don't seem to care about the crimes committed against nature in the name of the game. They see nothing offensive about a two-hundred-foot wall of cold concrete and glass looming over the fairways. How better to shield a tee shot from those pesky Gulf breezes? And, really, who cares about blocking out the horizon? Seen one sunset, seen 'em all.

Welcome to paradise, suckers. Prices start in the mid-400s.

Many of the top names in course design—Nicklaus, Robert Trent Jones, the Fazios—shy away from vertical monoliths in most of their developments. However, there's no escaping the fact that untold thousands of acres of wild habitat in this country have been sacrificed for the dubious cause of recreational golf. The one positive thing to be said about the proliferation of these projects is that, in fast-growing communities, the alternative can be worse.

Newer golf courses often use recycled water and less toxic fertilizers, and even the older layouts are relatively easy on the ecology compared to the waste and pollution generated by the average suburban housing development. Mapping eighteen or thirty-six holes requires large, contiguous expanses of open land. As a result, residential density levels in golf communities tend to be significantly lower than that of large-scale subdivisions. That's beneficial in a place such as

Florida, which is filling up at the absurdly self-destructive rate of almost one thousand new residents per day.

In a sane world, conscientious officeholders would have put a halt to this stampede by enforcing sensible growth-management laws. But in the corrupt, whore-hopping reality of Tallahassee politics, that hasn't happened. Growth-for-growth's-sake is the engine that drives the special interests controlling the legislature, and greed is the fuel. Except for the withering Everglades and a few state preserves, every last unspoiled acre of my home state is up for grabs.

Interestingly, the new-golf-course business isn't thriving so well in the rest of the country. In 2006, more courses shut down than opened in the United States, the first time that's happened in sixty years. The downturn hasn't yet affected the Sunshine State.

Whenever I see another golf club under construction (and Florida must have more per capita than anyplace else on the planet), I have to remind myself that the fate of that lost land might otherwise be two thousand new "zero-lot-line" houses, with roads, sewers, a freeway exit and almost certainly a strip mall. In a sad but ironic way, the boom in golf courses is actually keeping greener what's left of Florida. Loblolly pines and Bermuda grass are better than concrete and asphalt, and infinitely more hospitable to wildlife and humans alike.

Nonetheless, it's a mystery why anyone would want a house with a fairway running past the backyard. If you can afford prime golf-course frontage, you can afford to live on a lake, a river or a mountainside—settings with tranquil, natural vistas, where squadrons of riding mowers don't show up at dawn.

A woman who married an heir to a newspaper fortune once went out of her way to tell me that she and her hubby divided their leisure time among five homes, all located on championship golf courses. I restrained myself from suggesting that she needed a brain scan.

The Downhill Lie

Evidently, some folks' idea of easy living is to slurp martinis on their porch deck while brightly garbed strangers in cleats stomp through the shrubbery in search of lost balls.

Years ago I wrote a newspaper story about a retiree who, though not a golfer, had purchased a small condominium at a club in Pompano Beach. The fellow soon got fed up with duffers breaking his windows or topping tee shots into his flower beds, so he launched a one-man insurgency. Every time a golf ball landed in his yard, he'd scuttle out the back door and snatch it.

One morning he was intercepted by an uncommonly fleet-footed player, and there ensued an ugly confrontation involving swordplay with a driver. Lawsuits were filed, and shortly thereafter the ball stealer was informed that the condo association had initiated eviction proceedings. The man defiantly presented himself as a crusader for the civil rights of nongolfers and, when I interviewed him, proudly displayed his stash of purloined golf balls, which filled a hallway closet. I don't recall how the case was settled, but I've always wondered what led the old guy to imagine that he could live on a golf course and not have to contend with golfers.

As the commercials on the Golf Channel make evident, beer drinking and prostate problems are core components of the male golfing experience. Recently, in Oak Ridge, Tennessee, a family with a fairway view from their windows installed video cameras because so many golfers were stopping to urinate on their property. More than forty offenders were recorded hosing down the trees and flowers, and in some cases ignoring posted signs that implored them to hold their bladders. Because the club was public, the pissers were not expelled or even admonished by name. However, after the videotapes aired on television, the Oak Ridge city manager hastily announced a campaign to install extra portable toilets on the course.

That no homesites were being hawked at the Quail Valley Golf Club was a major lure. It meant there were no human neighbors to offend when nature called and, more importantly, no chance that I'd ever have to hit a 6-iron from the patio of a surly stranger.

Better yet, actual wild quails nested on the land at Quail Valley! Such truth-in-advertising is rare—and highly discouraged—in the Florida real-estate racket. The tradition among developers here is to name their projects after wild creatures that they've exterminated or chased away, typically fox, bear, falcon, hawk, otter or panther. Not far from where I grew up was a course called Eagle Trace, upon which no trace of an eagle could be found. This was entirely expected.

The few hardy critters that have adapted to human encroachment are considered too prosaic to be exploited for sales-marketing purposes. The last time I checked, there were no luxury golf developments called Possum Ditch or Rat's Landing.

Before applying to Quail Valley, the only sporting clubs I'd ever joined were notable for their genial lack of exclusivity; if your check cleared, you were welcomed with open arms. Quail was different. Not only was the check much larger, references were required.

My wife wasn't worried, but I figured we had no chance if anyone on the membership committee was familiar with my writing. With their acid humor and derailed characters, the novels could hardly be described as mainstream establishment literature. Worse, for twenty years I'd been writing a newspaper column that at one time or another had infuriated just about every big shot in the state, regardless of race, creed or political alignment.

Lately I'd been raging, as had many columnists, about the bloody fiasco in Iraq. Polls showed that most Americans had come around to the same point of view— that the war was a colossal fuck-up—but little Indian River County still stood largely behind the president. Almost everywhere else in the nation, disgruntled Republicans armed with razor blades were slinking out in the dead of night to scrape off their Bush-Cheney bumper stickers.

The Downhill Lie

Not in Vero Beach; not yet, anyway.

As we waited for our membership interview, I feared a prickly cross-examination. . . .

Didn't you once write that the vice president's pacemaker should be attached to a polygraph machine? And did you not also malign our commander in chief for "grinning like a Muppet" during a press conference about Iraq, and for conducting the war in a "delusional fog"?

But the meeting at Quail Valley turned out to be laid-back and totally painless. There was no steely-eyed screening committee; only affable Kevin Given, the chief operating officer, and he was gracious enough not to mention the columns or the books. It was more of a social chat than an interrogation—how long have you lived in the Indian River area? What do you think of the schools? Do any of your kids play golf or tennis?

Wisely I let my wife do most of the talking, leading Kevin to conclude that her charms vastly outweighed any of my as-yet-unrevealed personality disorders.

A few weeks later, the acceptance letter arrived; we were officially country clubbers. Now I had to go out and play that nut-cruncher of a golf course.

Day 117

My first lesson with Steve Archer, the director of golf at Quail Valley. He's mild and good-natured, as patient as a bomb defuser. Afterwards he fills out a note card for me to keep in my bag:

"Posture—less knee flex . . . Spine should tilt 90 degrees to golf club.

"Wider stance. Inside heels, shoulder-width apart . . .

"Arms + body work at same pace—time out right hand, club head and right side."

That's a lot to think about before hitting a golf ball, but I've got thirty years of rust to shake off. My goal is to play two or three times a week until I break 88, or rip a tendon trying.

Day 119

Freakishly, I manage to birdie that savage par-5 at Sandridge upon which I took a 9 two weeks ago. However, I quickly piss away the found strokes (and more), finishing the nine at 13 dismal strokes over par.

When I was young, I would have stalked off the course boiling mad after blowing so many opportunities. Today I merely trudge, which I choose to view as a sign of maturity, not fatigue.

Day 120

My first round at Quail Valley—and also my first time playing with a caddy, which has me nervous. I'm prepared to overtip shamelessly if I offend him with my cussing, or my game.

His name is Delroy Smith and he's from Kingston, Jamaica, where he played cricket and soccer. He is a calming presence and, more importantly, a diplomat. Having looped on some of the toughest courses in the Northeast, Delroy is familiar with American profanity in all its gerundives, and nothing I say draws a flinch.

For the first fifteen holes I avoid embarrassing myself. Then, on the 16th—a long par-3—I banana-slice a 4-iron into a water hazard on the adjoining hole. Next shot overflies the green into a different lake, and so begins the skid. I finish with a 97.

On an upbeat note, the new irons felt good. I also sank a fair number of putts in the four-to-six-foot range.

Delroy thinks I should be teeing off from the blue tees, not the shorter whites. When I mention this to Leibo, he suggests that Delroy might be having some giggles at my expense.

Day 126

I shoot 51 on the front side, which is the same score that Jack Nicklaus shot on the first nine holes he ever played. He was, however, only ten years old at the time.

Day 152

Big decision: Following Delroy's advice, I'm now hitting from the blues. The additional 365 yards translates into an extra two or three lost balls per round.

Today's outing is exceptionally nightmarish. To torment myself I keep a splash count: On the front nine: five drives in the water. That's a .555 slugging average.

At No. 10, my tee shot skips into a trap, then bounces into the lake. On the very same hole, I scorch a pitching wedge over the green and into a creek full of mutant, moss-eating carp. Prudently, I quit keeping score.

Tomorrow I have another lesson. I'm bringing a straight razor.

Turtle Golf

According to the posted handicap ratings, the hardest hole at Quail Valley is No. 4, a seemingly straightaway par-4 that measures a modest 387 yards downhill from the blue tees.

A deceivingly bucolic-looking creek borders the right side of the fairway. The waterway is populated by hefty turtles, mostly yellowbelly sliders, that enjoy crawling up on the bank to sun themselves; during the winter months, it's not uncommon to count six or seven of them basking together. From a distance they look like a garden of mossy old Army helmets.

Because I customarily slice my drive into their creek, the turtles and I keep an uneasy relationship. Despite having poor eyesight, they seem to sense whenever I step to the tee box, and they move into defensive positions as quickly as turtles are able to move.

The Downhill Lie

Their reaction likely stems from an incident one bright and breezy afternoon when I skied a shot directly into a pod of the snoozing sliders. As soon as I made contact, I knew where the ball was heading. Having owned turtles as pets, I realized it was pointless to yell "Fore!" or any other warning. They simply don't listen to humans.

So I stood there squinting into the glare, trying to track my doomed drive as it rainbowed toward the shoreline where the sliders slept. When the ball landed, it made a loud **tonk!** and bounced as if striking macadam; simultaneously a lone turtle went airborne, a sight not often observed in nature.

Fortunately, the reptile's armored shell did its job; the poor fellow was dazed but unhurt. He righted himself and briskly followed his companions as they trundled en masse off the bank, into the creek. The splashes looked from a distance like small explosives.

Not a single turtle could be seen when I arrived to search for my ball; all of them had remained submerged, holding their breath. Who knows how long they stayed down.

The sliders share the waters of the golf course with hundreds of tilapia, perch and exotic carp, which were imported to gobble the hydrilla and keep the shorelines tidy. Some of the fish have grown quite large, up to 15 pounds, and breed with exuberance.

During spawning season, the carp and tilapia use their fins to fan small craters in the sandy shallows where they deposit their eggs. Fiercely protective, they react aggressively when an errant golf ball lands in their nesting beds, as too many of mine have done. I'm not sure exactly how the fish remove the balls— perhaps they nose them off the ledges into the depths, or slap them away with their tails—but remove them they do. On several occasions I've had a shot trickle into a liquid hazard, yet when I reached the spot there was only a lone carp to behold, defiantly hovering on her nest.

Having found water on sixteen of the eighteen holes at Quail Valley, I've devoted considerable thought to both the price and quality of the golf balls that I use.

Choosing a brand wasn't easy. Except for their general roundness, the balls on the market today are radically different from the balata ones I played as a kid. The newer models soar higher and roll longer—which in my case ensures that a really bad drive goes deeper than ever into the woods (or farther than ever from shore), and is therefore less likely to be recovered. Hitting the ball longer gets expensive when you haven't learned how to hit it straight.

No less a slugger than Jack Nicklaus advocates reducing the distance of new golf balls by at least 10 percent. He believes that the extended yardage has altered traditional strategies of the sport, and diminished the specialized skill requirements for both amateurs and professionals.

The first time I smacked a drive 275 yards was a tonic for my fifty-three-year-old ego, since I'd never hit one more than 225 when I was a teenager. It's a cheap thrill that dissipates the moment you see a lumpy, hungover,

chain-smoking geezer waddle to the tee and—
between coughs—clobber one 300-plus.

More than a billion golf balls are manufac-
tured annually, and most end up lost. Each
type is engineered for certain performance
qualities, though the specifications are impressive only if you believe they make a difference. You can choose low-compression
balls or high-compression balls; dual-core
balls or single-core balls; balls that are meant
to bite on a dime, or balls that are meant to
run like a scalded gerbil.

One brand comes with a seamless cover
and a "speed elasticity core." Another has
hexagonal dimples, supposedly to reduce air
drag. The type that Tiger Woods hits is made
of four pieces and wrapped with three covers,
the innermost of which minimizes the spin
when smashed with a driver.

One ball company actually boasts of having
the "thinnest urethane-elastomer cover"—a
desirable feature for a condom, perhaps, but of
dubious benefit in a plugged lie in a greenside
bunker.

The Downhill Lie

I'd always thought that a good golfer could play well with any unscuffed ball, no matter what logo was on the box. Likewise, a lousy golfer would never find salvation simply by switching brands; the physics of a slice were inconquerable, whether the victim was a Noodle or a Nike.

So when I launched my comeback, I stocked up on mid-priced balls from companies I remembered from the olden days. Later, several excellent players, including a couple of pros, told me that selecting the right ball really is important, even for a high handicapper. They said that the stuff you read in golf-ball advertisements isn't just techno-crap meant to impress naive duffers; it's valuable, stroke-saving data. No two brands are alike, they said.

It was a fantastic excuse for me to start purchasing the most expensive golf balls on the market, Titleist Pro V1s, which are endorsed by many top touring pros. They get their balls for free, of course, while the rest of us pay about $48 per dozen, including tax.

Here's what I knew about the 2006 edition Pro V1, based on the helpful product information supplied by the manufacturer. It had:

A large, high-velocity 1.530-inch core.

A redesigned Ionomer casing.

Soft compression "for outstanding feel."

"Drop-and-stop" greenside control (the term "drop-and-stop" being proudly trademarked).

"Penetrating trajectory"—always a selling point for men of my age.

Last but not least, it had 392 dimples arranged in an "icosahedral design."

Although empirical evidence abounds that the number of dimples on a golf ball is meaningless, manufacturers proudly advertise it anyway. One might assume that they're charging customers more per dimple, just as computer companies charge for extra megabytes, but that's not true. For $20 a dozen, a golfer may choose from balls featuring 300 dimples, 333 dimples or 432 dimples, respectively. They all promise greater length, better spin control and a softer feel around the greens.

"To produce optimum lift and increased

carry for added distance," an outfit named Dimplit sells a ball stamped with 1,070 dimples. That's almost three times as many as a Titleist has, but be assured that the Dimplit doesn't travel three times as far.

Another heavily promoted factor in the aerodynamics of a ball's flight is how its dimples are configured. I'd never encountered the term "icosahedral" until I saw it in the Titleist promotional material. According to **Merriam-Webster's Collegiate Dictionary**, it means "of or having the form of an icosahedron."

An icosahedron is "a polyhedron having twenty faces," and there's the hitch: A golf ball that's truly spherical cannot be truly icosahedral, because plane faces are flat.

Among the shapes that may be icosahedral are pyramids, decagonal dipyramids, elongated triangular gyrobicupolas, metabiaugmented dodecahedrons, nonagonal antiprisms . . . but not spheres. Spheres, like balls, are always round.

For the sake of argument, let's say that my

golf ball is merely round**ish,** and that the face of each dimple is a tiny plane. For 392 of them to be set in an "icosahedral design" would be a difficult feat, because 392 isn't evenly divisible by the number twenty, and (as we now know) every icosahedron has twenty faces.

The makers of Titleists probably have a slick defense for their esoteric geometric claims, but it doesn't matter. Most amateur players don't give a hoot how the dimples are designed. If a ball flies straight and rolls true, who cares if it's got one enormous dimple or ten thousand microscopic ones? I'll keep buying the damn thing because, like all golfers, I desperately need to **believe.**

The 392-dimple ball that I adopted during relapse seemed like a good one, and I'm not getting paid a dime to say that. The folks at Titleist aren't stupid—an endorsement by a hack with my scurrilous credentials wouldn't boost sales even slightly. It might, in fact, produce the opposite effect.

In any event, there's nothing as sickening

in golf as the splash of a $4 ball in a ten-foot-deep lake. That's why I reverted to my high-school custom of deploying "water balls" on high-risk tee shots.

A water ball is any ball that you don't mind losing—preferably one for which you did not pay. Some golfers swipe balls from the practice range for use on water holes, but that's tacky. Besides, range balls take such a daily drubbing that they often lose their juice, and can be undependable on long carries.

The ideal water ball is an inexpensive yet unmarred specimen that you stumble upon while searching the rough for one of your own. These little gems go into a special zippered pocket of my golf bag, along with some lower-priced balls that I purchase at a discount sports store.

The theory behind using water balls is to provide the shaky player with a perverse sort of immunity. It's a known golfing fact that the odds of dunking a ball decline in direct proportion to its retail value.

This makes perfect sense, given the warped

and jangled psyche of the average golfer. I tend to take a smoother, more relaxed swing at a found ball because, what the hell, it's a freebie. More often than not, I'll clear the hazard with yardage to spare.

And the times I fail aren't nearly so aggravating, the sting of the drubbed shot being mitigated by the satisfaction of having just saved myself four bucks. That's the sort of pitifully contorted reasoning to which the insecure and inconsistent golfer clings.

Acquaintances who are excellent players deride the water-ball tactic, saying it fosters a defeatist attitude. They claim that taking a premium ball out of the sleeve and slamming it over a gator-infested lagoon builds character and self-confidence.

Well, I've tried that, and guess what? Hooking a new Pro V1 into the drink is like totaling a Testarossa while pulling out of the sales lot. It makes you want to puke.

Luckily, friends with connections at Titleist arranged for me to receive a couple dozen Pro V1s, which, because they were free, I fearlessly began to tee up on water holes. One set of balls even bore my initials, although they are difficult to read when submerged at depths greater than five feet. Perhaps the icosahedral design deflects the light off the lettering.

Once I realized how rapidly my freebie Titleists were disappearing, I transferred the survivors out of the water-ball pocket in my golf bag. Of particular concern were the monogrammed specimens, which I knew could be retrieved from the inkiest grave by eagle-eyed golfers wielding telescopic ball scoopers. I'd seen these characters in action, patrolling the banks and shorelines while they played, dipping their scoopers among the darting carp and cringing turtles. I imagined them chortling every time they salvaged a shiny Pro V1 stamped with "CH."

Less than half a dozen golfers at the club have those initials, but it's unlikely that the scavengers would try to track down any of us in search of the ball's rightful owner.

And even if they did, I'd deny it was me.

Day 153

Another promising lesson at the club with Steve Archer, after which I scribble furiously on blank index cards:

"too much lower body movement"

"practice with a baseball swing"

"time downswing with weight shift"

"on short irons, shift weight to the left; use right hand"

"Rotation—left shoulder over right knee"

"Setup posture, shoulder tilt more right"

"FINISH!"

Day 164

From a sarcastic e-mail to Leibo: "Shot a 49 yesterday on the front nine. No pars, four 3-putts—very inspiring."

Leibo responds: "Shot a 75 today with 35 on the back. Very inspiring."

My reply: "Rub it in. I almost killed a turtle with one of my drives."

The Downhill Lie

Day 165

From another e-mail to Leibo: "Sorry I missed your call. I was on the back nine at Quail, pouring gasoline on my nuts. I've now gone eighteen holes without a par."

Day 175

Four three-putts and innumerable stupidities on the back nine.

At some point my sand wedge comes helicoptering out of a bunker, well in advance of the ball. Fenia, who's riding along with me in the cart, wishes she'd worn a disguise.

Day 202

The pitfalls of Senior Golf—somehow I've hurt my back, and I can barely bend to tie my shoes.

Yet searing pain seems to be the antidote

for my swing ailments, because I knock the ball as straight as a cannon on the practice range. I decide to play nine holes and, despite the agony, I'm scoring much better than usual.

Then calamity strikes: For no good reason, my lumbar muscles relax on the par-5 seventh. I'm lying two, only eighty yards from the pin, when suddenly the pain in my back vanishes.

What happens next unfolds with a bleak inevitability. I skull a half-wedge into a sidehill bunker, overfly the green into the lake, and end up taking an 8, the dreaded "snowman."

And on it goes. . . .

Before every round I should have Fenia wallop me with a crowbar at the base of the spine. I play much better with tears in my eyes.

The Loneliest Number

Soon after my relapse, friends began lecturing me on the importance of establishing a handicap. This is a number calculated to rate a golfer's level of performance, under parameters set by the United States Golf Association. The higher one's handicap is, the more strokes that he or she is awarded toward par during a round.

The purpose is to enable mediocre players to compete evenly against much better players, a charitable tilting of the field that doesn't occur in most other sports. It's like giving a lousy bowler three extra frames to catch up.

A golfer with an astronomical handicap can shoot 95 and still take money off a low handicapper who shoots 80, which has always struck me as a somewhat hollow victory and not much to brag about. The pros typically play to positive handicaps (Tiger Woods' hovers around +8), meaning that in a friendly match they actually must **forfeit** strokes to par. It seems absurd.

I can understand the attraction of a mathematical formula that permits a duffer on his greatest day to "beat" a pro on his worst, but it dances around the rather glaring truth that the two of them don't belong on the same golf course together, much less in the same foursome.

The main reason I'd resisted handicapping my scores was that the system brands hackers such as myself with the numerical equivalent of a scarlet letter. This, I feared, would corrode my new, fragile truce with the game. I knew very well what a crummy player I was; double-digit documentation wasn't necessary.

Among sports, golf is uniquely driven by a quest for numbers that are low, not high. Many golfers don't always keep score, and on those days they're undoubtedly the happiest. Writing in **The Wall Street Journal,** Jeff Silverman argued eloquently for tossing out the scorecards and pencils, and he lamented the symptoms of "lead poisoning" that afflict so many of us:

"We become so hostage to the accumulation of the 2s and 3s and 4s and 5s we covet, en route to the 70s, 80s or 90s we aim for to validate our golfing selves, that the point of the pencil begins to leach into our swings. Our arms grow heavy. Our grips tighten. Our teeth clench. Our spirits sag . . . and our numbers spike like a fever."

Silverman described the liberating joys of numberless golf—the time freed for quiet reflection, bonding with nature and experimenting whimsically with new shots. It's an idyllic scenario, but back at the clubhouse somebody is bound to nail you with the most ancient question in golf: How'd you shoot?

And they'll expect you to cough up a number, not a sonnet.

When I was a teenager, my friends and I kept score although we never bothered to calculate our handicaps. There was no reason; being perpetually broke, we never bet when we played.

The grown-up world is different, I was warned. It's not cool to be guessing at one's handicap when cold cash is involved.

As it happened, I'd been saving my scorecards in order to track my progress, or lack thereof. Many of the outings were nine holes, because that's all I usually had time to play after work.

One June morning, after stern rebukes from Leibo, Lupica and others, I sat down at the computer and painstakingly began entering my scores online. When all the numbers were tabulated, I was stunned: My home course handicap was 17, and my USGA index was 14.2.

It seemed impossible, since I seldom shot better than 92, twenty strokes over par, and occasionally I ballooned above 100. When I complained to my friends that the computer had screwed up, they explained that the ranking system weighs a golfer's best scores disproportionately while discarding the worst.

"It's easy to bring your handicap down,"

Lupica said, "but it's much harder to make it go up. Don't ask me why."

According to the USGA, the handicap system "is based upon the potential ability of a player rather than an average of all his scores. . . . [The] average player is expected to play his Course Handicap or better only about 25 percent of the time, average three strokes higher than his handicap, and have his best score in 20 be only two strokes better than his handicap."

That was a surprise. Naively, I'd assumed that my handicap index would be the disparity in strokes between my average round and a score of even par. In fact, the method for determining individual handicaps is so convoluted that your head will split open like a bad melon if you try to decode it.

Of your twenty most recent golf scores, your ten lowest receive a "handicap differential," which is your "adjusted gross score" minus the USGA Course Rating (usually a couple strokes either side of 72), multiplied by 113 and then divided by the Slope Rating (somewhere between 55 and 155). The differentials are then averaged, and the sum is multiplied by .96 and rounded to the nearest tenth.

Wouldn't you love to know the handicap of the pinhead who cooked up that equation?

Another reason for my incongruously low handicap was the relative difficulty of the golf course, as indicated by the assigned Slope Rating. The USGA considers a slope of 113 to be of "standard" hardship. The course I play, Quail Valley, is rated 133 from the blue tees, meaning that a score of, say, 90 is weighted for handicapping purposes the same as a lower score on a less demanding layout.

If all that wasn't sufficiently confusing, it turned out that my handicap index was artificially suppressed because so many of my early scorecards covered only nine holes. As any bumblefuck knows, it's easier to play like a star for nine than it is to sustain a streak of competence for the full eighteen.

As is true in sportfishing, golf for some men is basically a dick-measuring contest.

The Downhill Lie

Lying inevitably occurs, some of it clever and some of it clumsy. Among true devotees of the sport, honor is prized because there are no referees or judges on the course; each player is relied upon to be truthful. Consequently, it's easy for a common shitweasel to nudge his ball out of the rough, cheat on his scorecard and churn those bogus pars into a lower, more impressive handicap.

That's the nature of many, though not all, clubhouse lies. A more cunning tack of deceit, I learned, is to present oneself as a worse golfer than one actually is. This is achieved by withholding your lowest scorecards, thereby falsely inflating your handicap. The hotly scorned practice, known as sandbagging, results in extra strokes being awarded to the dishonest player, enhancing his chances of winning and/or collecting on a tasty wager.

"Enter all your scores," Mike Leibick told me. "Good and bad."

And that's what I've done, with no small measure of pain and humility.

Day 209

It's taken seven months, but I finally break 90.

The scorecard is bizarre: three birdies, five pars, two bogeys, six doubles and two triples. I'm quite certain that I'll never again make three birdies in a round as long as I live.

Bill Becker's observation: "You hit the ball in places where you're in no danger of being in somebody else's divot."

Day 215

My first, and probably last, eagle!

Naturally, there are no witnesses. That's because I'm playing alone, as I often do, being pathologically terrified of embarrassing myself in front of other players.

The wonder shot takes place on the seventh hole, a par-5, where my drive slices to an adjacent fairway. I recover with a solidly struck 6-iron, though it lands in a yawning trap, 145 yards from the middle of the green.

I can't even see the flagstick over the manicured lip of the crater. Needing serious loft, I take a 9-iron and set up the way Bill Becker had once coached me, with the ball well back in my stance. Amazingly, I pick the shot so clean that hardly a grain of sand is disturbed.

Hurrying down the fairway, I scout in vain for a gleaming white speck on or near the green. I'm left to assume that the ball bounced over the putting surface and into the lake, which really pisses me off.

I search the shoreline, swearing viciously. The couple on the next tee are giving me an odd look, and I wonder if my long bunker shot nearly beaned them. However, they seem more amused than angry.

As I'm preparing to take a drop, a ludicrous thought crosses my mind. Just for the hell of it, I walk up to the pin and peek inside the cup. . . .

And there's my Titleist.

I know it's mine because of the Grey Goose logo—Leibo had sent me a box of freebies from Bacardi. I pluck the ball from the hole and euphorically scratch a "3" on the scorecard.

Thanks to the eagle, I end up shooting my best nine ever—a 41, and that includes a tragicomic 9 on the third hole.

My fifty-third birthday was a couple of days ago, so this is a nice present. I allow myself to imagine that I'm actually getting better at golf.

Day 238

Paul Bogaards, a good friend and big shot at my publishing company, arrives for a promised round at Quail Valley. The wind is blowing mercilessly from due east, and I'm swinging like a woodchopper.

On the fifth tee I do my famous Babe Ruth impersonation, pointing down the edge of the fairway to the precise location where my drive will veer over the watery ditch, out of bounds.

I take a big swing, and there she goes. Paul is impressed.

He cards an 89, while I gimp home with a 97.

Day 246/Los Angeles

Dinner with my friend Wil Shriner, the television and movie director. He introduces me to big Dan Boever, a professional stunt golfer and long-drive contestant. One of Dan's tricks is driving a ball through a piece of plywood. Another is hitting it three hundred yards with a putter.

He would be a fun partner for the next tournament at my club, although I'm not sure the other members would approve.

Day 256

Scorching hot and nearly dead calm. My card is 43-45 for an 88, after tripling the last two holes (including an ignominious four-putt on No. 18). Another clutch finish for The Kid. Whatever the reason—tiredness, tension or just nerves—I always seem to melt down on the home stretch whenever I'm playing well. It's uncanny.

Overall, though, it's been a good day, including as it did a surreal string of five consecutive pars. Once again I find myself encouraged, though a dark inner voice warns that I'm fooling myself.

Day 262

Sure enough: A swift descent into the bowels of hell. I lose seven balls in nine holes, which is the only score I keep.

With a northeast wind howling like Satan's own hound, every aspect of my game disintegrates. By the end of the afternoon, I'm too drained to kick the golf cart, much less bash it with my driver.

The Mystic Link

One day, after a particularly disheartening round, I turned on the Golf Channel and became transfixed by an infomercial touting a product called the Q-Link, a basic-looking pendant that was said to hold marvelous powers. According to the manufacturer, the device contained a special "resonating cell" that would "eliminate stress and improve focus" on the golf course.

The idea sounded so loony that I found it irresistible. The Q-Link Web site promised that the pendant would fortify my "biofield" and improve mental acuity. It was also a trendy fashion accessory: "Sleek and chic, with a dual-tone design, this beveled-edge triangle has two distinct sides, each making a unique statement. It can be worn by both men and women as a signature piece, dressed up or down. Designed by internationally acclaimed designer Neville Brody . . . the result is leading-edge attitude and super-charged power."

Brody is a hip young British typographer and graphics innovator, but nothing in his biography suggests that he knows squat about the stressfulness of golf. Nevertheless, I took the bait.

No sooner had I dialed the 800 number than the fellow on the other end clued me in on a hot deal—the solid gold Q-Link just happened to be on sale for $899!

"No thanks," I told him.

"The titanium model is available for $269," he said. "Today only."

"I don't think so." I ordered the Q-Link in basic black ceramic for $129, and contemplated what I would tell my friends if my golfing skills mysteriously improved.

Leery though I was, opening the package was still a letdown. "Golf's secret weapon" appeared to be a simple copper coil encased in plastic and attached to a very ordinary leather string. It looked like a bovine intra-uterine device.

The Downhill Lie

I looped the dorky thing around my neck, discreetly concealing it under my shirt, and headed for the practice range. Nothing mystical occurred except that I began hooking my metal-woods in a screaming, knee-high arc that defied Newtonian law.

Later, standing at the first tee box, I adjusted the lanyard to make sure that the coil was centered above my sternum, as the instructions recommended.

Then I took out my driver, addressed the ball . . .

. . . and promptly hammered it far into the nastiest patch of the heaviest rough. I double-bogeyed the hole, feeling as stressed out and unfocused as ever. I staggered through the front nine awaiting the promised embrace of serenity, but my Q-Link failed to resonate even faintly. I caught myself wondering if I should have sprung for the titanium upgrade.

I finished with a bruising 97 that included six three-putts and only two pars, a sorry-ass performance even by my sorry-ass standards. It was tempting to blame the $129 cow IUD around my neck, but I wanted to be fair. Perhaps I had deployed it improperly.

Upon returning home I carefully reviewed the instructional video that had come with the pendant. The presentation was made by a man named Robert Williams, identified as the Q-Link's inventor. Looking more like a Napa vintner than a scratch golfer, he explained that we each have unique life forces that are disturbed by electromagnetic frequencies from coffeemakers, microwaves, computers, televisions—presumably even the televisions upon which Williams's commercials are aired. He said that the Q-Link "harmonizes" these human biofields using a patented method called Sympathetic Resource Technology.

Inside the plastic triangle was more than just a coil of common copper; there was also a miniature tuning board and the aforementioned resonating cell. Williams asserted that more than twenty-five "scientific" studies had shown that the Q-Link had a salutary effect on stress, fatigue and even human blood. (According to a disclaimer, the device would not cure diseases or even minor medical problems, but I didn't care. If it could heal my putting woes, I'd deal with the arthritis.)

Among other useful facts provided by the company video:

- Unlike hypodermic syringes, your Q-Link can be shared with someone else and there are "no harmful effects."
- The Q-Link never wears out and is perfectly safe to wear twenty-four hours a day, even in the shower.
- Although most golfers keep their Q-Links around their necks, it may also be carried in the right-side pants pocket. However, studies showed that pocket placement is only 75 percent as effective, because the resonating cell is farther from your heart. (For the record, there's no claim of any sexual benefits while your Q-Link is in trouser mode.)
- Unlike Tinker Bell, the Q-Link "requires no belief for it to work." This

was a bonus for nonbelievers such as me, who would be inclined to think that the product was a complete rip-off.

Risking another dose of electromagnetic poisoning, I revisited the official Q-Link Web site and learned that twenty-eight touring pros had used the pendant during PGA competition, including Fred Funk and Mark Calcavecchia. How well these guys performed while sporting their Q-Links was not thoroughly chronicled.

A fellow named Ted Purdy won the 2005 Byron Nelson Classic while supposedly draped with a Q-Link, and several top money-winners on the Champions Tour (formerly the Seniors Tour) were listed as satisfied customers. In fact, the entire European Ryder Cup roster of 2002 was said to have been necklaced en masse on the road to victory. I assumed they got a bulk discount.

The next time I tried the Q-Link, I wore it

facedown to position the cosmic coil closer to my heart. According to the instructions, this method was entirely acceptable and, in fact, favored by many golfers.

It helped not even slightly. I still had five three-putts on the way to a 91, featuring a stellar 50 on the back side.

For two weeks I waited in vain for my stress levels to subside, and for my focus to sharpen. Although I didn't shower in my Neville Brody creation, or loan it to friends, I did wear it faithfully on the golf course, despite mild chafing. Its effect on my game ranged from indiscernible to adverse.

One afternoon, after making a hash of the 16th hole, I whipped off the pendant and vowed to get my money back. That evening, the following exchange took place between me and the woman who answered the phone at Q-Link HQ.

Q. Why are you returning it?

A. Because it doesn't work.

I mentioned my deplorable putting, but

she seemed unmoved. Your refund, she said, will be forthcoming.

No sooner had I transferred custody of the Q-Link to the United States Postal Service than I experienced an almost transcendental unburdening, as if a toxic mojo had been purged from my biofield.

Wishful thinking, as it turned out. My inner golfing frequencies remained hopelessly jangled with static.

Day 283

After hitting three consecutive 7-irons into the lake from the eighth tee, I suavely pick up and move on.

Day 289

I'm considering switching from the overlapping grip favored by Ben Hogan to the interlocking grip preferred by Nicklaus and Woods. I experiment by alternating on each hole.

Day 290

My first golf foursome in thirty-three years.
That sonofabitch Leibo talked me into it.
It's me, him, Al Simmens and a genial, mild-
mannered fellow named Bill Anderson.

Apparently, betting is involved. I assign
myself a Quail Valley handicap of 20, which
sounds about right. Leibo and I are paired
together and that's fine; he'll keep me
laughing. When I tell him that I've been
going back and forth between overlapping
and interlocking grips, he suggests
switching in the middle of my backswing.

Before teeing off, I dip into my small
stash of pre-flight Xanax. It might as well
have been a Tic-Tac, for all the good it
does. I shoot a ghastly 103; Leibo shoots
80. Somehow we still win the Nassau,
with a couple of side bets, and end up
splitting $26.

"How is that possible?" I ask.

"Just shut up and take the money,"
he says.

Day 295

I've officially switched to an interlocking grip, with no detectable improvement in either my driving or my long irons. However, my hands don't ache as much at the end of the day.

At Sandridge I shoot 50 on the front nine after being tailed for two holes by the ranger, who finally busts me for driving off the cart path on a par-3, which apparently is a Code Red violation.

All this I blame on residual bad karma from the Q-Link, still en route to the refund bin.

Day 297

I phone Lupica to vent about my terrible putting. He advises me to try a different putter.

"I can't do that," I say. "Fenia gave me this one as a present."

"You can always keep another putter on

the side," he says, lowering his voice. "She wouldn't have to know about it."

"It doesn't seem right."

"Keep it in your locker out at the clubhouse. She'll never find out," he says.

Just thinking about other putters makes me feel guilty. The Scotty Cameron is flawless and true, and I feel bound by loyalty. Yet there's no denying that a certain restless tension has crept into our relationship.

De-Grooving
the Waggle

One day I opened my locker and found a book titled **Golf Is Not a Game of Perfect,** by Dr. Bob Rotella. It had been placed there by a well-meaning caddy who, after watching me on the practice range, decided I was a head case.

Rotella is a sports psychologist who preaches positive thinking, calm acceptance and something called "fun." In the golf world he has attained guru status, thanks to accolades from Tom Kite and other successful pros.

I pored through the whole book, dog-earing pages. One of the most intriguing chapters is titled "Thriving Under Pressure," in which Rotella deconstructs the act of choking—a syndrome with which I am crushingly familiar.

According to Rotella, "A golfer chokes when he lets anger, doubt, fear or some other extraneous factor distract him before a shot."

Here, I thought, is the seed of the problem. Anger, doubt and fear are essential ingredients of my golfing philosophy.

Nervousness is different, Rotella explains. Nervousness can be good. He recounts that basketball legend Bill Russell always felt more confident about winning if he tossed his cookies before a big game. (Although I've never vomited before hitting a golf shot, I often feel like doing it afterwards.)

Rotella goes on to compare nerves on the golf course with what you feel before having sex with someone for the first time. "If it didn't make you nervous," he writes, "it wouldn't be so gratifying. In fact, it might be a little boring. Ask any prostitute." (The next time I see one on the driving range, I will!)

Toward the end of the book, Rotella distills his formula for winning golf into about three dozen rules about courage, confidence, concentration, composure, patience, practice, persistence, potential and, of course, the elusive f-word: fun.

"On the first tee," he writes, "a golfer must expect only two things of himself: to have fun, and to focus his mind properly on every shot."

Gee, is that all?

Admittedly, much of what Rotella says makes sense; most golf books do. I now own a shelfful of them, and a handicap that flutters up and down like a runaway kite.

Golf books and golf magazines sell like crazy because every player is searching for the formula, the secret, the code, the grail—how do I conquer this impossible, godforsaken game?

And the more you read, the more hopelessly muddled you become. After digesting an article by David Leadbetter advocating an early cocking of the wrists on the backswing, I came upon the following quote from the late Byron Nelson:

"Make a takeway with no wrist break, and you'll like what happens through impact."

Now what? Choose between Leadbetter, tutor of champions, or Nelson, the only guy to win eleven consecutive PGA tournaments?

Because no two experts play, teach or analyze golf the same way, the instructionals are often contradictory and vexing.

About a year into my relapse, I bought a copy of **Ben Hogan's Five Lessons, The Modern Fundamentals of Golf,** written in 1957 with the great Herbert Warren Wind. It was this classic text that a non-golfer named

The Downhill Lie

Larry Nelson picked up at the relatively advanced age of twenty-one, after returning from combat duty in Vietnam. By assiduously applying Hogan's methods, Nelson taught himself to play, turned pro, and went on to win two PGA Championships and a U.S. Open.

I am neither twenty-one years old nor blessed with Nelson's natural athleticism. Few amateurs are. Yet, early in his book, Hogan matter-of-factly tells of a businessman who came to him for lessons: "He was a 90-shooter in April. Five months later he was playing in the 70s and won the club championship."

The story probably was intended to be motivational, but it made me want to toss my golf bag in the Indian River. How do you cut 20 strokes off your score in only five months?

Hogan's student wasn't portrayed as an athlete-savant or even as a man of uncommon discipline, but rather a regular guy. Hogan believed that "any average golfer" who dedicates himself to learning the fundamentals "should be coming close to breaking 80 or actually break 80" within six months.

The program worked for his businessman-pupil back in 1938, as it did for Larry Nelson three decades later. It might have worked for me, too, had the instructions not been presented with such intimidating, and occasionally stultifying, technicality.

For instance, five full pages are devoted to the pre-shot "waggle," the key points helpfully emphasized by Hogan in capital letters:

EACH TIME YOU WAGGLE THE CLUB BACK, THE RIGHT ELBOW SHOULD HIT THE FRONT PART OF YOUR RIGHT HIP, JUST ABOUT WHERE YOUR WATCH POCKET IS. WHEN THIS TAKES PLACE, THE LEFT ELBOW, AS IT MUST, COMES OUT SLIGHTLY, THE LOWER PART OF THE ARM FROM THE ELBOW DOWN ROTATES A LITTLE, AND THE LEFT HAND MOVES THREE INCHES OR SO PAST THE BALL TOWARD THE TARGET. AS

The Downhill Lie

THE HANDS MOVE BACK TO THE BALL ON
THE FORWARD WAGGLE, THE LEFT HAND
ALSO MOVES AN INCH OR TWO PAST THE
BALL TOWARD THE TARGET.

With all due respect to Hogan, one of the
finest golfers of all time, I would suggest that
life is too bloody short to spend more than
ten seconds trying to decipher those direc-
tions. I'd also point out that any golfer who
labored so painstakingly on pre-shot machi-
nations would be pummeled unconscious by
his playing partners, probably on the first tee.

A meticulous fellow, Hogan was so serious
about his waggle that he provided not one
but two illustrations in the book, to show
exactly how it should be done. "The rhythm
of the waggle varies with each shot you play,"
he goes on. "DON'T GROOVE YOUR WAGGLE."

One cannot groove what one does not
have. My own swing begins with a tremor,
not a waggle, and that seems to suit my game.

The legendary Texas golf instructor Harvey Penick cautioned his students not to

become so fixated on waggling as to disrupt the larger task. As Penick pointed out, "The great Horton Smith used no waggle at all."

Reading that made me feel much better, which was Penick's speciality. With five million copies in print, **Harvey Penick's Little Red Book,** written with Bud Shrake, is the best-selling sports book in publishing history.

"Golfers are gullible," Penick himself noted, with the amused affection that flavors his writing. Short and anecdotal, the **Little Red Book** rambles fondly, like your favorite uncle sipping bourbon on the veranda.

When the book was first published in 1992, golfers devoured it because Penick's wisdom is bite-sized, elementary and never stern; he waxes with genuine empathy for the Sunday hacker. Since he learned the game in the era (and company) of Hogan, Nelson and Jimmy Demaret, Penick's advice can also be quaintly dated.

As one example, for swing training he buoyantly recommends "a common weed cutter" of the type once used by prison road gangs. Such implements were long ago supplanted in hardware stores by gasoline-powered, rotary-spooled yard trimmers that should never be swung like a 5-iron, unless you're aiming to strip the flesh from your shins.

The core of the Penick approach was unshakable optimism, a trait not native to the wintry Nordic soul. When Penick declares that "golf has probably kept more people sane than psychiatrists have," I can only absorb the remark as a commentary on the failings of psychoanalysis.

Golf books are like putts—the shorter, the better. For me, the most helpful ones are light on ruminations and heavy on the basics. **How I Play Golf,** by Tiger Woods, might as well be called **In Your Dreams, Sucker,** because no mere mortal can strike a ball the way he does. Still, the photographs in his book taught me more about the physics of a proper golf swing than anything else I'd seen.

Another good one is David Leadbetter's

Positive Practice, which also features excellent pictures. Like Tiger's book, Leadbetter's is large enough for the coffee table and written in language so simple that even Paris Hilton could make sense of it, were she ever to take up golf (or reading).

The key, of course, is in the execution. If the sport were so easy that any dolt could learn it from a book, all golf magazines would go bankrupt. They're not; they're thriving.

That's because most players drift from weekend to weekend in a fog of anxious flux; they play well in streaks and then, for no plain reason, fall apart. They are seldom more than one poor round away from stammering desperation, and to these unhinged souls every golf article dangles the most precious enticement: hope.

Whatever's wrong with your game, they say, it can be fixed. Just keep reading.

A sure way to transform yourself into a drooling halfwit is to scour a year's worth of golf articles, absorbing all the tips offered by Ernie, Tiger, Phil, Annika, Sergio, Butch,

The Downhill Lie

Hank or name-the-expert. Before long, you will actually feel the lobes of your brain begin to swell. Soon your ears are seeping and your eyeballs are bulging and you can't remember the alphabet, much less a helpful swing thought.

Naturally, I buy every golf magazine that I see and read it from cover to cover. Each issue promises a miracle cure for the slice, and one of these days I'll find one that works for more than two or three holes.

A sample of teaser lines from the stacks on my desk: How to Play with Consistency, How to Play the Shots to Win, How Phil Nails His Tee Shots, How to Putt Like the Best, How to Save Five Shots, How to Hit Great Shots from the Three Toughest Lies in Golf, How to Get Your Game Back, How to Master the Scariest Greenside Shot, How to Beat Your Fear of Forced Carries, How to Hit One-Hop-and-Stop Wedges, How to Break 100, How to Break 90, How to Break 80, and an article that presumably would annul the need for all others: How to Be Tiger.

One popular magazine is **Golf Digest,** which I paw through every month like a junkie in a medicine cabinet. It was there I found a health study reporting that 80 percent of all golfers have pains, illness or injuries, 27 percent have back problems and 30 percent have teed off with a hangover. The study also said that 66 percent of golfers are overweight, a figure that seems somewhat low, based on a casual census of Florida courses.

Dan Jenkins, probably the funniest sports journalist ever, writes a **Golf Digest** column that speaks to the cranky soul of every middle-aged hacker. It was he who implored golf-course designers to make sure all putts break to the left.

"There ought to be an easy way to do this, modern turf and drainage and bulldozers being what they are," Jenkins wrote. "Nobody can make a putt that breaks to the right. It's unnatural. Unless you're left-handed, of course."

As an editorial counterpoint to the stroke-saving tips, equipment reviews and humorous commentary, golf magazines always include at least one stealth zinger that's guaranteed to poleaxe your self-esteem.

The most unnerving golf fact I've ever seen in print: Justin Timberlake plays to a 6-handicap.

This is no joke. **Golf Digest** ranked the top one hundred musicians who golf as a hobby and, being a music fan, I'd skimmed the list with innocent curiosity.

Kenny G, who plays to a +0.6, is number one. That's all right, as I have no strong feelings about Kenny G's work; it's gotten me through many long elevator rides.

Interestingly, among musician-golfers the prevailing genre is country. Low-scoring stars include Vince Gill (0), Steve Azar (0.9), George Strait (8.4) and Kix Brooks (10). I've got no problem with those guys, either. Country music is fine.

Nor would I mind getting whupped on a golf course by rock legends such as Alice Cooper (5.3), Robby Krieger (6.8), Roger

Waters (11.7) or Glenn Frey (12.6). It would, in fact, be a trip.

Likewise, any player of my generation would be pleased to know he could unholster a shaky 15-plus handicap and tee off without shame in a foursome including Stephen Stills (15.1), Neil Young (18.6) and Bob Dylan (17). (Children of the Sixties might find it difficult to picture Dylan in a pastel pullover and two-toned FootJoys. Yet perhaps "Blowin' in the Wind" was never intended as a social anthem; perhaps Bob was waxing about the seventh tee at Pebble Beach.)

The list of golfing musicians was entertaining, but of course I couldn't enjoy it for the harmless celebrity froth that it was. No, I had to lock on to that single, ego-stomping tidbit:

Justin Timberlake plays to a 6.

Meaning that the former star of a hip-hopping, lip-syncing boy band can kick my sorry ass all over the links. That's harsh.

I own no 'N Sync CDs, nor can I name a single hit song that the group ever recorded (although I'm told there were many). I wasn't even sure who Timberlake was before he untethered Janet Jackson's left breast during that Super Bowl halftime show, an act infinitely more forgivable in my view than carrying a 6-handicap.

Emotionally, I can handle being a worse golfer than Engelbert Humperdinck (8.1), or Michael Bolton (10.1), or even—God help me—Pat Boone (14.8).

Not Justin Timberlake. Please.

True, by all accounts he's a decent guy. Loves animals. Sends roses to his mom on her birthday. He even hosts a PGA tournament that benefits the Shriners Hospitals for Children.

But he was in a freakin' boy band, okay? He **cannot** be such an excellent golfer. It just ain't right.

If the kid's fudging his handicap, he's not alone. The **Golf Digest** survey included a disclaimer saying that while some of the handicap indexes came from the USGA, others were provided by the musicians, their pals or publicists.

Snoop Dogg claims to be an 18, and who without a concealed-weapons permit would dare challenge him on that? On the other hand, when does Céline Dion (an alleged 16.8) have time for golf? She does, what— twenty-nine shows a week in Vegas?

You can definitely sniff PR weasels behind the scenes, overpromoting their clients. Yet even if Timberlake is an honest 10- or even a 12-handicap, that's still stunningly good golf for someone who sings falsetto and shaves with a cereal boxtop.

Golf Digest, which is keen on lists, also publishes an annual handicap sheet for the top two hundred CEOs of Fortune 1000 companies. As a group the CEOs are better golfers than musicians, which isn't surprising. Corporate big shots spend a lot more time on the course. Fifty-seven percent of those polled in 2006 said they play at least thirty rounds every year, which would be hard to do if one was touring with a globe-trotting boy band.

Three out of four CEOs said they've

shelled out as much as $300 for a green fee, while 45 percent said they belonged to four or more private country clubs. (It wasn't noted how many of those memberships were purchased for them by unsuspecting share-holders.)

Few CEOs in this country are young studs, but many of them golf like they are. In 2006 the number one scorer was fifty-two-year-old Jim Crane, head of a global freight company called EGL, Inc. His hand-icap index was 0.8, for which any twenty-five-year-old amateur (and even some pros) would kill.

In fact, of the top dozen CEO players, all but two were guys in their fifties who, except for their mountainous stock options and superb skills on a golf course, were not so dif-ferent from me.

A glass-half-full type would find it encour-aging that so many men in the same age bracket are playing top-flight golf. Plainly, it's not a physical impossibility.

But as a dedicated glass-half-empty person, my reflex reaction to the CEO list was dejection. My most dependable excuse for struggling so ineffectually to master the sport—age—had been demolished in print. The only straw left to clutch was the fact that most of those corporate single-digit handicappers hadn't abandoned golf for three decades the way I'd done.

This sort of pointless, self-excoriating meditation should be avoided by the average player. No wonder that Steve Archer, the pro who was teaching me, told me to throw away all my golf magazines.

One of these days I just might.

Day 319

Haven't touched the sticks in almost three weeks—the longest layoff since I started playing again. In the meantime, the Q-Link refund has shown up on the Amex bill, which can only mean (or so I tell myself) that its bad karma is vanquished and my golfing fortunes will improve.

Ha! I bungle and thrash my way to yet another ragged 97.

Back home, there's celebrity pillhead news on the Internet:

Upon returning to Palm Beach from a golf vacation in the Dominican Republic, radio gasbag Rush Limbaugh was detained by U.S. Customs for possessing a stash of Viagra prescribed in someone else's name.

Limbaugh, whose appetite for Vicodin had previously gotten him into a jam with Florida authorities, obviously moved to my fair state for the tax benefits, golf opportunities and friendly pharmacists. He has joined four country clubs here, so it's probably easier for him to get a tee time than it is to get laid.

Still, I'd be curious to know what effect, if any, the Viagra is having on Big Rush's USGA handicap, which is comparable to my own.

Day 321

For the first time since college, I walk eighteen holes dragging a golf bag. The heat index is 101, according to the weather station.

Last night the course got drenched with four inches of rain, so no carts are allowed. Several of the deeper sand traps are full of water, and I actually lose a ball in one of them, which is a first. I end up shooting 92—not sensational, but I'll take it under such arduous Saharan conditions.

Day 322

Lupica calls to say he caught Lyme disease from a deer tick that bit him while he was playing golf.

"You have ticks in your fairways?" I ask.

"Not in the fairways, you asshole. In the rough."

"I'm not sure I want to play a course that

has ticks," I say. "I'd rather deal with alligators."

Afterwards I wonder if I should have sounded more sympathetic.

Day 323

I take a putting lesson from the eternally patient Archer. He suggests trying a reverse-overlap grip, which seems to work. I hole a long birdie on No. 5 and finish the front nine at 43.

On the back side I stumble as usual, shooting 49. However, I par the gonad-shriveling 18th for the first time ever, which lightens the suffering.

Day 325

A new low: With a group of old high school friends, I rack up an execrable 104 at Riomar Country Club, one of the oldest courses in Florida. Afterwards I throw my visor in a trash can, in order to purge the evil mojo.

Tomorrow we play Quail Valley, and I'm scared shitless.

Day 326

Discarding the hat helped, except on the greens. My score is 93, with five three-putts. For a change, I strike the ball well off the tee, which is to be expected since I'm leaving for St. Augustine tomorrow to be fitted for a new driver.

Launch Control to Major Dork

Back in 1998, the Professional Golfers' Association asked the state of Florida for $50 million to help finance a project called the World Golf Village. Disguised as a sales-tax rebate, the giveaway was pro-rated at $2 million annually for twenty-five years.

Although the PGA was hardly hurting for dough, its request for government funding was quickly approved, the Florida Legislature being infamous for drunkenly throwing tax dollars at wealthy sports franchises. Between 1994 and 2001, $559 million in public money was earmarked to subsidize new pro baseball parks, football stadiums, basketball arenas, hockey palaces and even the head-quarters for the International Game Fish Association (an impressive place, if you're a fan of taxidermy).

Eventually Florida voters became pissed off about the tax handouts and the legislators got spooked, but by then the World Golf Village—basically a Disney World for golf fanatics—was already a done deal. Built on the outskirts of America's oldest city, St. Augustine, the project has an IMAX theater, an eighteen-hole putting layout, a teaching academy, two championship courses, a per-petual hole-in-one contest (first prize: two tickets to the Masters) and the World Golf Hall of Fame. The sprawling property has become a major tourist draw, and is spawning high-end housing developments on all sides.

Among the myriad attractions inside the World Golf Village is a retail megastore called the PGA Tour Stop, showcasing every upscale line of clubs, putters, balls, shoes and apparel. On the second floor is where a player can be measured, timed and fitted for a new club, or for a whole set.

"You **have** to go," Leibo told me. "I can't wait to see you on the launch monitor."

The launch monitor is a device of modern invention used by golf-club sellers to electronically analyze the swings of potential customers. In my case, I'd be tested on a driver, the most difficult club in the bag to hit. It's also the most expensive club in the bag, because frustrated golfers—which is to say, all golfers—are eternally shopping for a new model.

I asked Leibo how the launch monitor works.

The Downhill Lie

"You hit some balls into a net, and a machine measures your clubhead speed, the ball spin, the launch angle, everything. It's unbelievable," he said.

I told him that I'd reached an age at which I really didn't want my launch angle measured.

"I'm going to call today and make an appointment," he said brightly. "We'll drive up there together."

A few days before the trip, I started experiencing launch-performance anxiety.

"What if I can't make a decent swing?" I said. "You know how badly I play when strangers are watching."

Leibo told me to relax. "You'll hit about sixty balls. There's bound to be one or two good ones."

For moral support, I phoned Lupica, who'd recently purchased a high-tech Ping driver after being assessed on a launch monitor.

"It'll change your life," he assured me.

Leibo and Al Simmens accompanied me

to the World Golf Village for my Thursday afternoon club fitting. We arrived an hour early and purchased some golf shirts at the PGA Tour Stop.

Then I retrieved my Callaway Big Bertha from the car and we headed upstairs to the testing bay.

"Ask for Keith," Leibo said. "I told them you'd need somebody with a sense of humor."

While Keith was finishing with another customer, I practiced hitting a few balls. The net was so large that it was impossible to miss. It was also impossible to tell where the shots were going.

Keith came in and observed me for a few minutes before introducing himself. He placed one of the balls on a rubber tee in front of the launch monitor, a compact camera-like box mounted at a level slightly below my knees.

"Give it a try," he said.

I hit several in a row, while Keith studied a color monitor that displayed a flurry of numbers and three-dimensional shapes after every shot. His expression was that of a cardiologist staring at a flatline EKG.

"You're hitting it hard left," he reported, "**really** hard left."

"That's weird. I usually have a big slice."

"Well, that last one was twenty-seven yards left of center," he said, "and some of the others were worse."

I glanced at Al and Mike. They were sitting in patio chairs, enjoying every ugly minute.

"You did hook a few the last time we played," Mike reminded me.

"That first grouping got a zero rating," Keith said, which meant the shots were so wildly scattered that there was no statistical pattern. "I don't think I've ever seen a zero rating before," Keith remarked, shaking his head.

And where, I wondered, was his famous sense of humor?

Gamely I hit a half a dozen more drives, but Keith remained pensive. He called in another pro to review the results.

"How bad is it?" I asked.

"Have you thought about taking up fly-fishing?" Keith asked.

"Or maybe bowling?" said the other guy.

They pretended to be kidding. A second color monitor displayed the computer-imagined path of each of my drives on a simulated fairway—the white lines wriggled hither and yon in a chaotic tangle, as if someone had detonated a plate of linguini. A few of the shots flew so low to the ground that they had no measurable launch angle at all.

"That's awful," I said, and not even my friends disagreed.

A third club fitter arrived to join the huddle around the tracking equipment, and by now it felt like I was observing my own autopsy. The consensus in the testing room was that my hands were rolling over before impact, turning the face of the golf club inward before it struck the ball.

So I checked my grip, realigned my stance, slowed my downswing and gradually started

launching the ball—thwack, thwack, thwack—
to a well-frayed spot in the net.

Watching the display screen, Keith perked
up. "Your angle of attack is good," he
reported. "So's your ball speed and your spin
rate."

"What's his clubhead speed?" Big Al asked.

Keith said it was 98 mph, which is great
for a fastball but only slightly above average
for an amateur golf drive. Keith sent one of
the other pros to get a couple of drivers with
different shafts.

"Yours is too stiff," he explained.

"That's not what his wife says," Leibo vol-
unteered from his patio chair.

The other clubs didn't swing any easier
than mine, but the data from the launch
monitor indicated that I was striking one of
them higher and straighter. To prove it, Keith
took me out to the range, and forty minutes
later I was the proud owner of a new $399
Callaway Fusion with a regular flex shaft.

The club was only six cubic centimeters
larger than my Big Bertha 454, and had

barely a half-degree more slant to the face. Nonetheless, I was irrationally hopeful that the new purchase would cure my chronic problems on the tee.

Unfortunately, the shop was out of Callaway Fusion drivers with the specifications I needed. Keith said he'd ship a new one in two weeks.

On the long, winding road out of the World Golf Village, I realized that I hadn't screwed up the nerve to ask what my launch angle was, or what it was supposed to be.

Knowing, I suspect, would not have sent my confidence soaring on gilded wings.

Day 330

The day after subjecting myself to the launch-monitor experience, we tackle the Palencia, a scenic but tricky course north of St. Augustine. I score atrociously, yet I drive the ball fairly well with the Big Bertha—so well that I'm having regrets about ordering that new driver.

The Downhill Lie

Day 332

I'm flabbergasted to learn that players at my handicap level aren't permitted to take a score higher than a 7 on any hole, according to the rules of the United States Golf Association. That means I shot an adjusted gross of 100 the other day, not 103.

For some reason I don't feel like turning cartwheels.

Day 336

Back at Quail Valley, I smack a once-in-a-millennium 4-iron to within thirty feet on the treacherous 18th hole . . . and smoothly three-putt for a bogey.

Later, on a whim, I pick up the phone to track down David Feherty, the brilliantly twisted golf analyst for CBS. We've never met or even spoken, but I've heard through mutual friends that he's read some of my novels. I locate him on the road, between tournaments, and he listens with great patience but evident concern to the story of my golfing relapse.

"The only real mistake you can make is caring," he says. "Don't worry, though, I'll get you detoxed and then you won't give a shit."

"I feel like quitting again every time I play," I admit, "then I hit one good shot, and all I want to do is go out and play again."

"Yeah," Feherty says sympathetically, "it's like a drug."

Day 338

I haven't broken 90 in three months, and it might never happen again. I seem stuck on the desolate plateau of mediocrity that has claimed so many golfers.

My USGA handicap index is now 15.6 and rising faster than Floyd Landis's sperm count.

Day 339

I hit six greens on the front nine, birdie No. 7 after a shockingly efficient lob wedge, and still make the turn at 42, thanks to several feeble three-putts. True to form, I crumble on the back nine and slump off the course with a 92.

One sunny note: I was even on the par-5s.

Gulag California

While vacationing with my family near Laguna, I ventured to a daunting seaside links course called Monarch Beach. The hotel concierge had assured me that I could play a late round alone; otherwise I'd never have left my room. The idea of golfing with strangers on a strange course was mortifying.

I paid the green fees, rented some clubs and

hit a few balls into a net. Then I checked in with the starter, who cheerfully announced that I'd be paired with another player. I broke into a sickly sweat, but it was impossible to back out of the game—the guy was standing right beside me, putting on his glove.

He was a stocky, amiable fellow in his forties whom we will call Mel, some sort of account executive from Tennessee. I smiled gamely, but on the inside my gut was torquing. I was **not** ready for this.

When the starter turned and waved in another direction, I tasted bile. "We're gonna put you guys with two other singles," he said to Mel and me. "You don't mind, do you? Have a great round!"

Whereupon we were introduced to Craig and Don. Craig was tall and athletic-looking, also in sales. He sported cantaloupe-colored bell bottoms, which I could only assume had snuck back into style.

Don was no less fit, though more reserved and less festively attired. He and I shared a cart, which was equipped with detailed GPS mapping of the entire course. The overhead screen displayed precise yardage from the cart location to all major hazards, as well as the greens. I'd never golfed with the assistance of orbiting satellites, but Don seemed familiar with the technology.

The starter screaked a yellow Sharpie across our scorecard, highlighting the many holes upon which we weren't allowed to drive off the cart path. I gave the wheel to Don and crept off to call my wife, in the craven hope that one of the kids had sprained an arm or possibly split a lip while surfing—nothing dire, just serious enough to give me a plausible excuse for bolting.

Fenia didn't answer her cell, so I whispered an urgent message: "I'm trapped, honey! They stuck me with three other guys and I can't weasel out of it!"

Back at the starter's box, I noticed with alarm that my new companions were drifting toward "the tips"—the black, or championship, tees.

According to the scorecard, Monarch

Beach measures 6,601 yards from the black tees and has a Slope Rating of 138, which is cowing to a golfer of my stunted abilities. On the other hand, my home course was 6,540 from the blues, so, I reasoned, how much tougher could it be?

After inquiring about my handicap, Mel said, not in a transparently condescending tone, "You probably want to play from the whites."

I'd like to believe he was sincerely trying to spare me some embarrassment, but the **machismo** gene clicked on. "That's okay," I said, "I'll just hit from wherever you guys are hitting."

There was nothing to lose. Apparently I'd already been pegged as the duffer in the group, and nobody was betting any money on the round.

Still, teeing up in front of three younger, vastly more experienced golfers was a bowel-wringing experience. It didn't help that I was the only one wearing sneakers and playing with rented sticks.

The Downhill Lie

Then something strange and unexpected happened: Mel yanked his first drive into a hill near the out-of-bounds markers, while I pounded mine straight down the middle of the fairway. My new companions seemed as surprised as I was, and implicit in the tone of their congratulations—and my acknowledgment—was the certainty that my shot was merely a happy fluke.

I bogeyed that first hole, but so did they. As we waited on the next tee, Craig asked Don what his handicap was.

"Zero," Don replied.

"Wow."

"I used to be a teaching pro," he added. "I've still got my PGA card."

Perfect, I thought. I'm partnered with a professional. Without further ado, I stood up and launched a screamer hard left. The ball struck a tree—possibly numerous trees—before caroming out of the shadows near the cart path. The other guys spanked perfect drives.

That's how the afternoon went, good holes and bad holes, the usual roller coaster. Nonetheless, I managed to hang in there with Craig and Mel; Don, as expected, was kicking our asses. Every now and then I'd ask for a tip—how to carve a wedge off a downhill lie, for instance—and he'd respond politely but not expansively. Clearly his teaching days were over.

Play was brutally slow because the course was jammed. The cart restrictions rendered the GPS range finder practically useless, since everyone had to schlep on foot across the fairways to reach their balls. On these treks, Craig, Mel and Don each brought a veritable bouquet of irons, so as to be prepared for any distance and any possible lie.

Not having so many shots in my bag, I usually grabbed one club. Sometimes I guessed right and sometimes I guessed wrong. Often it was the proper choice, struck poorly.

On the sixth hole, by sheer dumb luck, I knocked a 9-iron about eight feet from the pin and sank the putt for a birdie. I proceeded to double-bogey the seventh, par the eighth, then mutilate the par-5 ninth to finish the front at 46.

All things considered, I felt all right. I hadn't scored nearly as wretchedly as I was capable of. Still, it was a relief to hear Don say that he wouldn't be able to play the back nine because he had a long drive back to Palm Springs. Briskly I chimed in with an alibi of my own—an adoring family, waiting back at the hotel.

Mel and Craig waved so long and headed for the 10th tee. I shook Don's hand and wished him a safe journey. Then I scurried into the bar for a Coke.

It had taken two hours and thirty-five minutes to play those nine holes—a death trek for a golfer debilitated by social reticence and acute swing-thought anxieties. Yet somehow I'd endured—hitting from the tips, no less—without the aid of sedatives or booze. No tirades, seizures, casualties or collateral damage.

The first round of the British Open had been played earlier that day at the Royal Liverpool Golf Club, and the group in the bar was still buzzing about a spectacular shot that Tiger Woods had made on the 14th hole.

That night I caught the replay on ESPN—a blind 4-iron, 209 yards straight into the cup. I recalled the hilarious 4-iron that I'd hit on the ninth at Monarch Beach that afternoon—arcing high into a Pacific headwind before stalling like a decrepit warbler, then plummeting into a pond.

For the remainder of our vacation I avoided the golf course as if it were a toxic dump, although I awoke early every morning to catch the live Open coverage from Liverpool. When Woods broke down on the 18th green after winning the tournament, I got choked up, too. His grieving for his late father made me think of mine.

Tiger and I have nothing in common except that neither of us would have picked up a golf club if it weren't for our dads. Tough old Earl Woods surely would have been beaming at the sight of his supernaturally talented son collecting an eleventh major championship at the tender age of thirty years.

I can't be certain what Odel Hiaasen would think of me, his eldest offspring, slashing and cussing my way around a golf course again at age fifty-three. I suspect he'd be pleased that I was trying.

Day 351

A sleek new King Cobra Speed driver arrives, courtesy of Feherty, who has a commercial deal with the Cobra line. I rush out to the range and instantly start launching balls at a trajectory that resembles a space shuttle blastoff. The new club has a loft of 10.5 degrees, which is plainly ill-suited for my swing.

Later, UPS delivers a box from the Callaway company—the Fusion driver for which I'd been "fitted" at the World Golf Hall of Fame. Giddy with anticipation I'm not.

Day 353

Nine dismal holes with the Fusion.

It's weighted for a fade, which would be helpful if I was still snap-hooking the ball as I did that day on the launch monitor. Unfortunately, my slice has returned in a breathtaking way, exaggerated to farcical effect by the expensive new driver.

I receive an e-mail from Lupica: "I'm trying to shorten my swing."

"Yeah," I write back, "and I'm trying to shorten my memory."

Day 356

The new **Golf Digest** features a full-page advertisement for "Mind Drive," an herbal capsule that supposedly clears the brain and dramatically improves one's golfing abilities.

From the promotional material: "Mind Drive helps keep you calm and focused so you can concentrate on your game, eliminate distractions, increase consistency and lower your score."

The ad doesn't reveal the ingredients in this wondrous product, but rousing endorsements are offered by Ryan Palmer, D. A. Points and Vaughn Taylor, three young PGA touring pros. The most well-known blurber is Phil Mickelson's one-time swing coach, Rick Smith, who's quoted as saying: "Mind Drive ensures you get into the Zone, taking your game to the next level and achieving consistency."

Oddly, Mickelson himself doesn't chime in on behalf of Mind Drive, nor does his name appear in advertisements for the miracle capsules. It's hard to believe that Smith wouldn't have told his star pupil about this exciting breakthrough, especially after Mickelson's heartbreaking collapse on the final hole of the 2006 U.S. Open. Maybe Phil has a different coach for homeopathic consultations.

I dial the 800 number for Mind Drive and order sixty capsules for forty bucks.

The guy on the other end offers to sign me up for the lifetime home-delivery program, but I tell him that I'll wait to see if the stuff really puts me in "the Zone."

The Q-Link fiasco is still fresh in my mind.

Days 358–360 / Bridgehampton, New York

Mike Lupica has invited me to the Noyac Golf Club, where he's a member. The slope from the whites is a challenging 138. The course is very pretty, the slender fairways bordered densely with old oaks, and not a tract house in sight.

Among these woods is where Lupica was assaulted by the Lyme-carrying tick, but that's the least of my worries. I'm off to a terrible start, swinging like a lumberjack, which is appropriate since I spend most of the morning in the trees.

The Downhill Lie

At one point we encounter the course superintendent, whom Lupica engages in a lively dialogue about the length of the rough, which Mike feels is unduly punitive. I don't hear the entire exchange, but it ends with the superintendent threatening to fire off a letter of complaint to the club big shots about Lupica's smartass attitude. Mike doesn't seem especially worried.

The back nine begins more promisingly, with me nearly sinking a fifty-foot blast from a sidehill bunker. Then comes the customary Hiaasen choke. Blessedly, Lupica and son Alex seem to have quit keeping score. I three-putt so many greens that I disgustedly bag the Scotty Cameron and borrow Mike's putter, with positive results.

Of the three drivers in my bag (out of pity, Lupica has waived the fourteen-club rule) the most useless in my hands proves to be the Fusion for which I was fitted at the World Golf Hall of Fame. I can't hit the thing worth a damn. However, young Alex

Lupica borrows it and knocks the ball a mile, straight and true. He is also sixteen years old, an age at which all things are possible.

The next afternoon, Lupica loans me a freaky blue Ping putter, which works pretty well for nine holes. When we're done, Lupica insists that I drive one ball off the 10th tee with his beloved G5. To our mutual astonishment, I crush it 272 yards, according to the markers on the fairway sprinklers. Now I'm completely confused. Should I add a Ping driver to my growing collection?

Late the following afternoon, we head out for one last masochistic nine at Noyac. This time we're joined by Mike's eldest son, Chris, who has the ideal outlook for golf— it's all comedy, so why take it seriously? I scrape out a 44, which isn't bad.

Afterwards, in the pro shop, we watch Tiger Woods sink a birdie to win the Buick Open with his fourth straight 66. Of all people, Rudy Giuliani walks in the door and snaps at his playing partner, who's glued to the television.

The former New York mayor is a new member at Noyac, and will soon be running for president of the United States. The arduous campaign is not likely to improve his handicap index, currently hovering around 18.

Outside, in the parking lot, we spy Giuliani's jet-black Escalade, the driver catching some Zs while his boss tackles the back nine. Before zipping my clubs into the travel bag, I present the fade-weighted Fusion to Alex Lupica. His dad hands me the blue Ping putter, and we call it even.

Later, in the shower, I check myself for ticks.

Day 363

Back in the familiar confines of Quail Valley, I par five out of the first six holes. Then I pull my usual crash-and-burn on the back nine, carding big fat 7s on No. 10, No. 17 and No. 18.

I finish with a lackluster 91, the toll including four dispiriting three-putts. The blue Ping let me down, or perhaps it's the other way around.

Still no sign of the Mind Drive pills in the mail, but Feherty has generously express-shipped another Speed Cobra driver, this one lofted at 9.0 degrees.

At this point I'd be willing to try a slingshot.

Day 364

Ominously, clouds of turkey buzzards have appeared at Quail Valley and the air is ripe with death. Because of the extreme summer heat, some of the jumbo carp and tilapia have floated up dead in the lakes, attracting hungry vultures from as far away as downtown Orlando. It's a good day to aim clear of the water.

I shoot 46–44 with eight pars (including

the tough 17th), two triples and three doubles. I'd been cruising toward breaking 90 when I was once again slaughtered by No. 18—four-putting the cruelly tiered green for another closing 7.

Overall, though, it wasn't a horrific day. Except for that last hole, the Ping putter performed honorably. I also drove the 9.0 Cobra fairly well, so I make a note to call Feherty and thank him.

Day 365

Steve Archer says I'm tilting left on my setup, which can cause, among other disasters, a hard pull. At the end of the lesson he also suggests that I test-drive a Nike SasQuatch 10.5, which looks like a deformed eggplant. I swing it once and smash the ball out of sight, which is scary.

Should I stick with the new Cobra or not? If only I had some Mind Drive pills to help me decide.

Later, on an impulse, I pick up the

phone and order a device called the Momentus Swing Trainer that's being advertised on the Golf Channel. According to Fred Funk, it will forever groove my swing.

We shall see.

The Anniversary Stomp

Exactly one year after I purchased those secondhand Nicklaus clubs, my transformation was disturbing.

I owned two pairs of golf shoes and a half-dozen vivid shirts in which I wouldn't have been caught dead twelve months ago. I had four drivers of varying lofts, weight distributions and shaft flexibility, and I couldn't hit any of them the same way twice. I was trying out a flashy new putter that I was concealing from my wife, and I found myself conversing about gap wedges and fairway hybrids with persons I barely knew. At nights I lay awake reliving the day's round, shot by shot, in self-lacerating detail.

A case could be made that I was hooked. Whether or not my game had actually improved was debatable, because I played in schizoid streaks that drew dumbfounded exclamations from even my most diplomatic friends. Nonetheless, after twelve months I was, at least on paper, where I'd hoped to be.

The USGA defines "a male bogey golfer" as "a player who has a Course Handicap of approximately 20 on a course of standard difficulty. He can hit tee shots an average of 200 yards and reach a 370-yard hole in two shots at sea level."

By those magnanimous criteria, I qualified. My Course Handicap stood at 18 on a layout of higher-than-average difficulty. My tee shots, when they found the fairway, traveled 245 yards to 275 yards depending on the wind and turf conditions. Unless waylaid by water or waste bunkers, I could easily reach (and often overshoot) a 370-yard hole in two strokes. In sum, I had reached a level of play at which I'd assured my friends and loved ones that I would be content.

Yet I wasn't. Every golfer is susceptible to the notion that he or she is scoring far beneath their potential, and many go to their graves clinging to this fantasy. The cruel truth is that most of us bog down in a stratum commensurate with our talent, mental fortitude and fitness.

Men of a certain age choose not to believe they've peaked, and I wasn't alone in this delusion. The mass-advertisers who aim at golfers know well their target demographic— and it ain't Orlando Bloom or Jake Gyllenhaal. Before I started playing golf again, I'd never even heard of Flomax; I thought a "weak stream" was a trout creek in autumn.

But flip open any golf magazine or turn on the Golf Channel, and you're peppered with medical remedies for enlarged prostates, high cholesterol, arthritis pain and erectile dysfunction. Obviously, millions of guys like me are out there, laboring valiantly to piss, make love and whack a small white ball as well as we did when we were young. That four-hour hard-on about which we're forewarned in the Cialis commercials is daunting to contemplate, but personally I'd be thrilled to keep my putter working for that long.

And I mean my putter.

As the mortal clock ticks down, the window of opportunity in which it's physically possible to post a memorable golf score grows narrower. I'm reminded of this in the dead of night when awakened by the twinge in my bad knee or the irksome throb in my right hip, which I fear will someday require surgical attention. Many people play the game until they're quite old and they have a blast, but par inevitably becomes a stranger. The trick, as David Feherty says, is learning not to care.

But care I do. The most insidious thing about golf is the one or two fine moments that it bequeaths every round. On my one-year anniversary I stumbled to a dreary 96, thanks to a feud with the new Cobra driver. A neutral scanning of that uninspiring scorecard would show nothing whatsoever to celebrate.

Yet instead of fuming about the five shots that I'd stupidly knocked into the water, I kept replaying in my mind's eye the impossible sidehill wedge that I'd nearly holed from the rough on No. 8—unquestionably a freak event, yet I chose to appraise it as an omen of future glory.

That's the secret of the sport's infernal seduction. It surrenders just enough good shots to let you talk yourself out of quitting.

Day 367

Leibo says my borrowed SasQuatch driver looks like a bicycle helmet on a stick. He advises me to make up with my Big Bertha. I do as he says, and rip the next five drives straight as an arrow.

"Know what your problem is?" Leibo muses. "You're a psycho. Your head explodes out here."

As for my huge and complicated blue putter, he says it resembles a psychedelic spatula. For further humiliation, he calls Al Simmens on a cell phone and describes the big Ping in detail.

Big Al asks: "Does it scale fish, too?"

Despite the insults, I'm sticking with the beast for now.

Day 371

The Medicus swing-training driver, the Mind Drive capsules and my USGA membership card all arrive today, which is either High-Octane Golf Mojo or a meaningless coincidence.

Day 372

Before surrendering my meditative wavelengths to Mind Drive, I scan the ingredients listed on the box: Vitamins B_1, B_6, B_{12}, folic acid mixed with "decaffeinated green tea extract" and a list of substances that I don't recognize. My wife urges me to Google the one called L-phenylalanine, but there's no time. I gulp two capsules and head for the golf course.

Playing the back nine first, I open with an encouraging par-5 on No. 10, a hole that usually is bedeviling. Before long, though, I lurch into an awful string of triples and doubles. I recall Mind Drive's claim to "enhance muscle memory" so that you can repeat the same golf swing, and it occurs to me that this might not be the ideal prescription for someone with a flawed swing.

On the second nine I start out par-birdie-par. After five holes I'm even, and beginning to believe that the Mind Drive potion might indeed be magical. Then play stacks up, and a congenial older gentleman asks to join me. I'm stunned to hear myself say yes, because I know damn well what's about to happen.

And it does: I three-putt the next two holes, dump two balls in the water on No. 8, and finish off the round with a spectacular, out-of-bounds 5-iron that lands no fewer than 80 degrees left of my intended target.

Even herbal medicine is no match for the Big Choke.

Day 373

After gulping down two more Mind Drive capsules, I go online to research L-phenylalanine. Medical Web sites say it's a protein amino acid that is widely believed to be a natural antidepressant.

Perfect for golf!

But there's lightning and thunder outside, so I stay home to watch the third round of the PGA Championship. At one point, ten players, including Tiger Woods, are tied for the lead.

The phone rings—my mother calling to make sure I've got the television on.

"I've never seen such great golf!" she exclaims.

Mom is seventy-nine, and she hasn't swung a club since PE in college. However, she has become a major Tiger fan, and keeps up with the big tournaments. She's especially excited that the PGA is being played at the Medinah Country Club, in her hometown of Chicago.

It's pretty adorable, and also ironic. If anybody has a reason not to be enamored of golfers, it's my mother.

Blue Sundays

Dad was a workaholic and our family seldom went on trips, even for weekends. Although we lived in a suburb of Fort Lauderdale, I can't remember my father ever joining us at the beach. He loved offshore fishing but the rest of us got seasick in rough weather, which is of course the best time to troll for marlin and sailfish.

Consequently, we usually opted for terrestrial activities. In those days, rural Broward County had no malls or video arcades, so my friends and I spent most of our free hours exploring the Everglades, fishing for bass or catching snakes.

On Saturdays, Dad either headed downtown to his law office, or worked on legal briefs at home. Sundays were for golf, period. My father would disappear early, leaving Mom alone with the kids all day. Over time she developed an understandable resentment toward Dad's golf, believing (not unreasonably) that he ought to hang out with his family at least one day of the week.

Like many boys, my main motivation for taking up golf was to have more time with my father. A second and less noble reason was to weasel out of going to church.

Dad was a laconic agnostic while my mother was, and still is, a devout Roman Catholic. Early in their marriage he'd agreed to let her raise us in the faith, which meant we had to attend catechism classes on Saturdays and Mass (in dreary, droning Latin) on Sundays— the entire weekend basically shot, from my point of view.

Escape beckoned in the form of Dad's golf excursions. I had noticed that his regular tee time coincided fortuitously with the mid-morning Mass at St. Gregory's. If Dad took me along to the club, I reasoned, then I'd have an excuse to skip church.

It seemed like a no-brainer. Golf couldn't be **that** hard to learn, I thought to myself.

Oh Lord, was I wrong.

My inability to master the game stung more sharply because of the friction that my new hobby was causing at home. Mom was perturbed because I was dodging Mass, and she felt that my father was abetting the enterprise. My little brother was too young to fret over such things, but I'm sure my two sisters were envious because I got to spend Sundays with Dad.

As frustrating as those outings often were,

The Downhill Lie

I don't regret a moment spent golfing with him. I do regret my conduct, swearing and fuming and blowing up over bad shots. Had I known that Dad would be gone from our lives so soon, I wouldn't have spoiled those days by acting like such a jerk.

Although he wanted me to love the game as much as he did, we weren't wired the same way. I was impatient, hotheaded and self-critical—the worst possible disposition for a golfer. Usually I'd pick up my ball before the round was done, and Dad would let me drive the cart the rest of the way. At that point all the pressure was off, and I have wonderful memories of sitting at the wheel, watching my father swing a driver with a sweet, fluid rhythm at which I could only marvel.

Looking back on those weekends, I can't help but feel sorry for my mother, locked out of such an important part of her husband's world. She was a golf widow long before it became a cliché. Considering the arguments that took place in our house on Sunday mornings, Mom would seem an unlikely fan of the game.

Yet she is. When I broke the news that I'd started playing golf again, she said it was a great idea. During my next visit, she gave me some black-and-white photographs of Dad that were taken by one of his aunts in the summer of 1942, when he was sixteen.

In the pictures he's tanned and lean, his hair blond from the sun. One snapshot shows him blasting out of a bunker; in another, he's pitching to a green. There's also a backlit photo of him holding the pose after hitting a fairway iron—hands high, hips fully rotated, belt buckle square to the target.

My father had one of the loveliest golf swings I've ever seen. Mom says the same thing. Although I'll never be able to play as well as he did, the photographs are a sentimental inspiration. They're tacked to the corkboard in my office.

The Downhill Lie

Day 375

At the Sandridge Golf Club, the muni where I'd taken my first midlife golf lessons, I am walking down a hill to retrieve my ball from a pond on the 12th hole of a layout named, for self-evident reasons, The Lakes.

From over my shoulder I hear a disconcerting squeak that sounds like nothing so much as chassis springs. I spin around just in time to see my golf cart roll into the water with a concussive splash.

Frantically I wade in as it slides toward murky and uninviting depths. I clamp both hands on the bumper and dig my heels into the muck and, astoundingly, the cart glugs to a halt. Gingerly I scramble aboard, struggling to lock the same fickle brake pedal that I'd thought I had secured only moments earlier.

No luck. The port side of the Club Car is listing precipitously. I flip the gear lever into Reverse and mash down the accelerator, which is now submerged.

Bubbles rise.

Wheels spin.

My heart sinks.

Moving to the rear of the cart, I hastily unstrap my Callaways and hurl the bag up on shore. Then, moronically, I brace my legs and try to drag the vehicle backwards. It doesn't budge an inch, but my right knee makes a noise like peach pits in a nutcracker.

Defeated, I retreat to dry land, dig my cell phone out of the golf bag and call John at the pro shop. I describe the situation and, after a thoughtful silence, he promises to send help.

In disgust I kick off my spikes and empty out the water, silt and hydrilla weed. Luckily the course is empty, and not a soul witnesses this abject tableau.

Soon, two golf carts speed to the scene—the ranger and the starter. Although they seem sympathetic, neither of them leaps out to assist in what is clearly going to be a challenging salvage operation.

"See if you can back it up," the ranger suggests.

I wade back out to the cart and, hanging like a stagecoach bandit on the sideboard, I manage to locate the gas pedal with my left foot.

More bubbles.

The ranger and the starter can be overheard discussing the possibility of my being electrocuted. "Better watch it," one of them calls out helpfully. "You might get a shock."

Quickly I return to shore, whereupon the ranger says, "Oh, could you go get the key? Just in case some kids come by and haul it out—we don't want anybody stealing it."

"Sure," I say, and slosh as casually as a gator poacher back into the flesh-sucking ooze.

Afterwards, the starter kindly offers up his golf cart so that I may finish my leisurely round. "This one is so slow," he says, "you can't get in any trouble."

Like I was drag-racing when I dunked the other one.

"My shoes are wrecked, so I'll have to play barefoot," I tell the ranger. "Don't report me."

He smiles patiently.

The accident severely disrupts my focus, and I run off a string of sloppy, unmemorable bogeys. One errant shot lands in heavy palmetto scrub, the favored habitat of diamondback rattlesnakes, so I'm forced to lace on my slimed, sodden golf shoes before pursuing the lost ball.

By bleak fortune, the 17th fairway parallels the opposite shore of the pond in which I'd shipwrecked the golf cart. Squishing up to the tee box, I'm greeted by the sight of a Jeep Cherokee (undoubtedly a V8) with a cable strung tautly from its rear rumper to my half-submerged chariot. The leaking cart being hauled from the brackish soup looks like a scene from CSI:

The Downhill Lie

Miami. All that's missing is David Caruso, squinting icily at the perpetrator: Me.

It's an unnerving interlude, but I rally—smacking a rescue club 190 yards down the throat of the fairway, then knocking a pitching wedge up on the island green, twenty feet from the pin.

Lining up a possible birdie, I hear the approach of another golf cart. It's John, my friend from the pro shop, delivering a damage report. I retell the whole story, apologizing profusely.

"The same thing happened when I set the brake near the 11th hole," I say, "but that time there wasn't any water around."

"The mechanics think they can get the cart running again," John says, "if they can hose all the mud out. If they can't . . ."

I nod gravely. "Just send me the bill."

"This isn't the first time this has happened," he adds consolingly. "I mean, it doesn't happen a lot—but it has happened before."

"But not often."

"No. Not very often," John says.

He waves and motors away. My birdie attempt rolls three feet past the hole.

I can't sink a putt, but I can sink a damn golf cart.

Day 376

"You are such a putz."

It's Leibo, calling for the highlights of the golf-cart episode. "Did you do this on purpose?" he demands.

I tell the whole embarrassing story.

He says, "I'm totally impressed that you continued playing. Most people would have quit."

"In all the years you've been golfing, haven't you ever sunk a cart?"

"Not once," he replies. "Not close. Not ever."

Lupica beeps in on call-waiting.

"Tell me it was a victimless crime," he says.

"I was alone in the cart. Nobody died." I grind through another recap.

The Downhill Lie

"Wait a minute—you went back into the water after it happened?" Lupica is incredulous. "You weren't worried about the alligators and snakes?"

"I had to get my clubs."

"You know what this means? You're a golfer now!" he declares. "You didn't even think about the gators—you went in to save your clubs! This is a huge rite of passage."

I ask him the same question I asked Leibo: "Haven't you ever sunk a cart before?"

"I've played golf since 1960," Lupica replies. "Nobody I know has ever drowned a golf cart."

"It wasn't completely underwater," I point out.

"Could you see the roof?"

"Absolutely. What do you think I was hanging on to?"

"That's the cover of your book!" he crows. "I can see it now."

"I don't think so."

"Oh, this is epic," he says.

"Can they eighty-six you from a public course?" I ask.

Lupica isn't sure.

Later I speak with my Mom, who wants to chat about Tiger's remarkable final round in the PGA. Then she asks, "So, how's your golf going?"

"Not so good. I sank a cart yesterday."

"Sank a cart?

"Yep."

"How'd you manage to do that?"

As soon as I begin the story, I hear muffled laughter on the other end.

"At least you took off your shoes, right?"

"No, Mom, I didn't have time."

More laughing.

"How deep was the lake? Did the cart go all the way under?" she asks.

"No, I grabbed the back bumper and held on."

Momentarily, my mother collects herself. "So this was quite a little adventure you had."

"Yeah, you could say that."

Rodent Golf

I have a history with vermin.

For years I kept red rat snakes, so named because of a specific culinary preference. The hundreds of rats that I fed to my pets were domestically bred, but they were rats nonetheless; basically the same tenacious flea-friendly critter that in the Middle Ages decimated Europe with the bubonic plague.

Several months into my golfing comeback, a rat chewed to shreds the auxiliary wiring harness in the underchassis of my Chevy Suburban, causing the air conditioner to more or less flame out. The gluttonous destruction was achieved on nighttime forays during the summer, while the vehicle was parked in the driveway of a house that my family and I were renting.

The cost of the rat noshing: $2,196.92.

Astonishingly, my insurance company agreed to pay for most of the damages. I was

informed that rodents in Florida regard auto-
motive wiring as a delicacy, and claims such
as mine were not rare.

Nonetheless, the inconvenience was aggravating. I'd been driving my SUV back and
forth to the golf course several times a week,
clueless to the nocturnal sabotage. Never
once had I spied a rat lurking near the Suburban, or anywhere in the yard.

Anticipating a repeat attack—and diminished sympathy from the insurance company—I was eager to locate the culprit before
he commenced snacking on my replacement
wiring.

The summer vacation ended without further incident. Then, on the day the kids went
back to school, I finished breakfast and
went outside to a shed where our appliance
boxes were stored. I found the box I needed,
opened it—and immediately spotted a
funky-looking nest made of shredded packing material, from which protruded a long,
twitchy black tail.

Hastily I shut the box and dashed into the

house in search of a weapon. There were two choices, both of which I'd purchased because of commercials on the Golf Channel. The first was the Medicus dual-hinge driver, endorsed by Mark O'Meara; the second was the Momentus Swing Trainer, endorsed by Fred Funk.

I'd been practicing sporadically with both devices, though my golf had not improved perceptibly. The Medicus is about the same length as a regulation driver, but the clubhead is rigged to waggle on a hinge if you make a mistake at any one of six compass points in your swing. It's an effective training aid, but to do battle with a wild rat I needed a bludgeon that wasn't going to flop impotently at the critical moment of impact.

So I grabbed the Momentus, basically a foreshortened 6-iron that's weighted heavily to build muscle strength. It has a molded grip for the hands, a sturdy steel shaft, and it tips the scale at a formidable 40 ounces—a full half-pound heavier than Barry Bonds's baseball bat.

What happened next wasn't pretty, but

save your postage stamps. A rat is nothing but a rat, okay? They're dirty, destructive, disease-carrying pests; as a species, the opposite of endangered. When the icecaps melt and the oceans rise, I promise you that billions of rats will be nesting safely in the treetops, warm and dry, making more rats.

Truthfully, there's no humane way to get rid of the bastards. The traps you buy at hardware stores painfully snap their bones. Poison causes their stomachs to explode. Cats just gnaw off their heads and then toy with their writhing corpses.

As a universal rule, rats are not euthanized; rats are exterminated. It's been that way since the beginning of man.

I had to make a split-second decision, and I have no regrets.

The Momentus golf trainer turned out to be ideal for mortal combat with feral rodents in close quarters. Three of the razor-toothed intruders were hiding in that cardboard box, and I waxed two of them. Admittedly, mine wasn't a textbook swing plane—more Lizzie

The Downhill Lie

Borden than Sam Snead—but I kept my head down, held my left arm straight and followed through to the target, which (unlike a golf ball) was hopping and thrashing and snapping at the clubhead.

Afterwards, while I was hosing the blood and fur off the hosel, it occurred to me that Fred Funk probably never envisioned the Momentus being deployed for such a mission. I considered dropping him a short note, with a sunny blurb for future infomercials:

"Forty ounces of rat-smashing power! I highly recommend the Momentus swing trainer for anyone trying to groove their golf swing, or battle a stubborn vermin infestation."

One lucky stiff escaped the hail of blows on that August morning, leaping clear of the mangled box and making a charge at my wife, who shrieked and slammed the porch door. Before I could give chase, the rat disappeared into the shrubbery.

If it's the same one that gnawed the wiring out of my Chevy, I hope we meet again. I'll be waiting, **chico,** me and my leetle friend.

Day 377

Sheepishly I call Sandridge for an update on the wet cart. To my relief, John reports that the mechanics have cleaned out the muck and gotten the engine running.

"Did they check that brake?"

"Yeah, it wasn't quite right," he says. "I think they changed the pads."

Vindication? Or is he just being polite?

"What do I owe you?" I ask.

"Nothing," he replies. "Just don't put another one in the lake, okay?"

The Tiger Beat

For me, the only thing more nerve-wracking than golfing with strangers is boarding airplanes with strangers. Or boarding alone, for that matter. Or with 250 nuns, each of them saying a Rosary.

The Downhill Lie

I'm not and never will be a carefree flier, but when duty calls I'll grit my teeth, inhale a Xanax and step up to the plate.

David Feherty had asked me to tag along with him inside the ropes at the Bridgestone Invitational, which is held at the legendary Firestone Country Club in Akron, Ohio. The purpose of the trip was to observe up close the level of divine skill at which professional golf is executed—an experience guaranteed to validate my own futility about the game.

According to MapQuest, the driving distance from my home in Florida to the front gates of Firestone was 1,072 miles, too far for a weekend road trip. So, on a Friday afternoon, the second day of the tournament, I courageously headed to the airport and medicated myself as prescribed.

The skies in the Midwest were stormy, so the flight was gut-heaving and miserable despite the sedation. I lurched off the plane and beheld downtown Akron, beckoning like Paris in a drizzle; no traveler has ever been so relieved to set foot in the former tire-and-rubber capital of the Western World.

At the golf course everyone was buzzing about a 9-iron that Tiger Woods had hit from the woods along the 18th fairway. The ball had traveled 212 yards, aided by a cartoon-like bounce off a cart path, and ended up briefly on the roof of the clubhouse though technically not out of bounds. Apparently at Firestone you can hook one all the way to Toledo and still escape a penalty stroke.

A conclave of PGA officials met while a lengthy search ensued. (A cook who was standing on the loading dock had innocently picked up Tiger's ball.) Eventually Woods got a free drop, chipped creatively to the green and nearly holed the putt for a par. The proceedings took thirty-two minutes, a soul-grinding eternity even for the most avid fans. Tiger finished the round with a 64, and as usual he was leading the tournament.

While Feherty taped the CBS highlights show, I chatted with another popular commentator, Gary McCord, who still competes on the Champions Tour. When I told him about my attempted comeback, he suggested that I take on a "real challenge" and try to qualify for a seniors amateur tournament. I informed him that things weren't going nearly that well.

"I sank a golf cart the other day," I confessed, "in a lake."

"Oh, I've done that," McCord said matter-of-factly.

"You have?"

"Yeah. We were chasing a roadrunner."

This was music to my ears.

The next afternoon, armed with network credentials and a cumbersome portable monitor that displayed the live network feed, I followed Feherty to the practice range, where Woods and his caddy were stationed distantly at one end, by themselves. We did not approach. Nobody did.

Feherty prowled the tee area, muttering to himself and greeting the other pros with "Hey, asshole" and other graphic endearments that unfailingly caused the players to grin or crack up. Despite giving the impression of being authentically miserable—he recently quit drinking—Feherty is one of the wittiest, most likable companions you could find. He's also uncommonly wise about golf and, although he claims to despise the sport, can be heard to say in unguarded moments, "I love to watch these guys hit the ball."

During his playing days Feherty won ten tournaments worldwide, and was a member of the 1991 European Ryder Cup team that dueled the Americans in the so-called War by the Shore at Kiawah Island, South Carolina. When asked why he retired from professional competition, Feherty said he saw a young rookie named Eldrick Woods hit a tee shot in Milwaukee and thought: "I've got to find another line of work."

He took a broadcasting job with CBS, penned a hilarious golf novel called **A Nasty Bit of Rough,** and now writes a column for **Golf Magazine** that is refreshingly blunt and occasionally raunchy.

After pacing the Firestone practice area,

The Downhill Lie

Feherty alighted near Ernie Els, who'd pulled a driver out of his bag. "Watch," Feherty whispered to me.

Els owns the Perry Como of golf swings, smooth and oh-so-easy, but the impact off the composite clubface sounded like a high-caliber rifle shot. The ball vanished on the fly over the back fence of the driving range.

I turned to Feherty and said, "Okay, I'm quitting golf again. This time for good."

Practicing next to Els was one of the tour's top young players, Adam Scott, who was rocketing one 3-iron after another down-range. All these guys are staggeringly good, and television doesn't do justice to their talents. Watching them swing, I was simultaneously awestruck and discouraged. My ball flight in no way resembled theirs, and I didn't need Stephen Hawking to tell me why.

Woods and Davis Love III teed off at 2 p.m. sharp, with Feherty and me in brisk pursuit. The Firestone South course is famously long and lushly maintained, and the stroll would have been lovely if it weren't for the gummy, sweltering weather. Feherty sullenly reported that he was in gastric distress; still, he traveled the fairway like it was carpeted with hot coals, and keeping up was a challenge. Behind Tiger and Phil Mickelson, he is arguably the third-biggest celebrity at PGA tournaments. Fans hollered his name constantly, and tugged at him for autographs.

"My constituency—drunken white guys," Feherty grumbled in mock annoyance. "I'm a magnet for morons."

Wielding the monitor, which the CBS crew had affectionately dubbed "the Turd-hurdler," I tried to appear useful when in reality my only interest was scoping out Woods. Having never seen him play in person, I didn't want to miss a trick.

And there were no shortage of those. On one hole he choked down on a 7-iron and cozied it 145 yards, a low draw to an uphill green. On the very next hole he took the same club and knocked it 215 yards, a high fade over the treetops.

"He's a freak of nature," Feherty said

admiringly. "The hundred-year flood. Maybe even the five-hundred-year flood."

Woods had finished first in his last three tournaments, including the British Open and PGA Championship, and was earning approximately $2,500 per stroke. At age thirty he'd already won fifty-two times on the tour, including twelve majors, and banked $63 million in prize winnings.

Some fans gripe that Tiger's dominance has made professional golf boring, but excellence isn't boring. Nobody ever turned off the television when Hank Aaron was at the plate, or when Dan Marino was dropping back in the pocket. Woods is the rarest of media phenomena, an athlete who lives up to the hype and surpasses it. He's done for golf what Muhammad Ali did for boxing and Michael Jordan did for basketball—attracted millions of new fans to a sport that desperately needed a spark.

Every player on the tour should drop to his knees and thank God for Tiger. Since he turned pro in 1996—in truth, **because** he turned pro—the amount of PGA prize money has tripled. The golfer who finished dead last on the Sunday scoreboard at Bridgestone would pocket $30,750, a nice paycheck for four days' work.

As it happened, a dubious blip of history occurred on the front nine: Tiger carded four straight bogeys, something that hadn't happened to him during a tournament in ten years.

"This is my fault," I told Feherty after Woods' second bogey. "All my bad putting mojo—it's probably wearing off on him. Maybe I'm standing too close."

"You fucking Norwegians," Feherty groaned.

But after the fourth bogey, his skepticism evaporated. "Jesus, Hiaasen, I think you're right!" he exclaimed after Tiger missed another short putt.

"We call it the Nordic pall of gloom," I said.

Once leading the field by two strokes, Woods was suddenly five down. Feherty was itching to ask him what was wrong, but Tiger's stare would have made a suicide bomber wet himself.

The Downhill Lie

After Woods birdied the 10th, Feherty sensed an opening. As we hurried along the 11th fairway, the Irishman sidled over to the world's greatest player and said, "What was goin' on back there, mate? All of a sudden you turned into a 12-handicapper."

Woods smiled ruefully. "I **wish** I was a 12-handicapper. I suck."

Feherty and Woods have a cordial relationship, partly because Feherty makes him laugh. In the heat of a tournament Tiger seldom speaks to anyone except Steve Williams, his caddy, yet he doesn't seem to mind the occasional profane zinger that Feherty fires his way.

Before the day was done, the other leaders faltered and Woods rallied to stay in the hunt. He made another birdie and finished only one shot behind Stewart Cink.

Rain was predicted for the next day, so the starting times were moved two hours earlier. That meant CBS would pre-tape the final round and broadcast it later, in the usual afternoon time slot. Feherty foresaw chaos, and blamed me for the oncoming monsoon. Nevertheless, he took mercy and decided I wouldn't be required to lug the Turdhurdler around all day. Instead I was issued a live headset as a prop, and ordered not to utter so much as a syllable into the microphone, under penalty of castration.

Woods, who was playing with Cink and Paul Casey, got off to a sluggish start. The booth announcers, Jim Nance and Lanny Wadkins, speculated that Tiger was getting tired after battling to three consecutive victories.

Listening on his headset, Feherty rolled his eyes. He didn't believe that Woods was fading. "He'll find a way to win if you give him a hockey stick and an orange," he said.

Sure enough, the birdies began to fall, and soon Tiger's name was on top of the leader board. He was shaping golf shots as gorgeously as Eric Clapton bends the notes on a Stratocaster. On one monster par-5, Woods pushed his drive into some thick rough in the maples, a gnarly lie from which most pros would have humbly chipped back toward the fairway.

Tiger never considered it. He shredded the heavy grass with a supercharged 3-iron, cutting the shot first around the outreaching limbs, then high over a distant stand of oaks and then finally across a pond before dropping it five feet from the flag, where it trickled to the fringe.

Feherty lowered his microphone and shook his head. This was golf as art.

Yet Cink lurked stubbornly, dropping clutch putts as storm clouds gathered to the west. Tiger missed a four-footer for par on the 16th, Cink birdied the 17th and they both finished at minus 10.

A tie meant a sudden-death playoff, and Feherty was roiling. The sky was turning purple, and he was booked on an early-evening nonstop to Dallas. "It's all your fault," he hissed at me. "The Norwegian curse."

The first three holes were a survival contest, Woods and Cink scrambling to match bogeys and pars. As soon as the players teed off on the fourth, the heavens of northern Ohio unloaded.

With rain pelting his face, Tiger calmly pulled out an 8-iron and through the squall fired the ball eight feet from the pin. Cink dumped his shot in a bunker, Woods rolled in his birdie and the soggy marathon was over.

"Finally," sighed Feherty.

He hopped into a waiting cart and, with me clinging like a gibbon to the rear bumper, the driver sped toward the CBS sound trailer. There Feherty hastily shed his microphone and harness, and bid farewell to the crew members, whom he would not see again until the new broadcast season in January.

Before bolting for the airport, Feherty asked if I needed any more clubs from Cobra.

What I needed, after watching Tiger play, was a bowling league.

Day 385

Halfway through the front nine, I run for cover as the thundering remains of

The Downhill Lie

Tropical Storm Ernesto shut down Quail Valley. I've made exactly one good shot—a full wedge that stopped five inches from the cup on No. 3. Everything else was Hack City.

I also seem to have misplaced my Mind Drive concentration capsules, a clue that they're not working as advertised.

Day 386

In the disarray of my office I find the blister pack of Mind Drives, and gulp two caps before driving to the course. Soon I start feeling jumpy and flushed. Sweat is dripping off my visor and landing squarely on the blade of my putter—I might be sick, but at least I'm properly centered over the ball.

Another lightning storm chases me off, but not before I execute some spectacularly wretched golf. The lowlight is losing two balls on No. 5 before smacking a large

4-iron to the green and sinking a twenty-five-footer to "save" double-bogey. On the par-3 eighth, I push two tee shots into the lake before hitting a 6-iron fifteen feet from the flag. Coolly I miss the putt and take a 7.

New theory: Whomping those rats has screwed up my swing.

Day 388

The Cobra 9.0 and I have reconciled, so Big Bertha is being exiled to my locker at the club.

"They have ways of getting out, you know," Lupica says darkly.

The neon Ping putter seems to be bailing on me, as well. To add to my aggravation, the apparatus has so many peculiar curves and sharp angles that it's impossible to get it clean with a golf towel. I need to take the blasted thing to a car wash and have it detailed.

The Downhill Lie

Day 390

"This game is fluid. It's always changing. It's always evolving. I could always hit the ball better, chip better, putt better, think better. You can get better tomorrow than you are today."

This is Tiger Woods, speaking to reporters after firing a 63 to win the Deutsche Bank Championship, his fifth tournament victory in a row. He's played his last twenty rounds at a stupefying 86 under par, yet all he talks about is improving his golf game.

If that doesn't motivate me, nothing will. Over my last twenty rounds, I'm approximately 438 over.

Day 391

A new personal worst—I accrue five 7s on my way to a drag-ass 96. So much for the miracle Mind Drive pills. My stepson says he wants to try them while he's doing his homework.

Go nuts, I tell him.

Day 392

Scotty Cameron and I are pals again—no three-putts today! As Lupica would say, this is epic.

However, I still shoot 91, thanks to a waterlogged quadruple bogey on No. 8 and a sandy triple on No. 12. Maybe one of these days I'll put it all together for one good, steady round.

Dream on, schmucko. Where does this lunacy end?

Six months from now, Quail Valley holds its annual Member-Guest Invitational, which I've been talked into entering by Peter Gethers, my book editor and a fellow hacker. Conveniently, Peter will remain far from the scene of the crime.

Why I succumbed to such an ill-starred

proposition is hard to explain. The idea of mingling with ninety-five other golfers, much less competing against them, conjures cold-sweat nightmares. I still get cramps on the practice range, for God's sake.

But, like many writers, I function better on a deadline. Unless I set a firm date and a goal, my exhumed struggle with golf might drag on until the onset of senility, and with it this journal. Twenty-four weeks seems a fair span of time in which to elevate my game to a semi-respectable level, or declare defeat. The Member-Guest will be either my Normandy or my Waterloo, but pivotal it will be.

Leibo has agreed to play in the tournament as my partner, but he has one demand: "Promise me you'll have fun."

Fun isn't such an abstract concept when your handicap index is 5.2, as is Mike's.

The club tournament will be set up as five nine-hole matches over two days, undoubtedly with wagering. I'm already twitching like Mel Gibson at a Kinky Friedman rally.

Day 394

Quinn Hiaasen, age six, is hauling his golf bag to the range. He carries only a driver, an 8-iron and a pitching wedge, all of which he deploys with enviable gusto and glee.

For me it's a new type of paternal experience, because I never got to golf with my older son, Scott. During my long hiatus from the game, he played for a few years and then quit. He says that I bought him a set of sticks in college, which is possible.

Now he's married, with three young children and a busy newspaper job in Miami. We're lucky if we get to fish together a couple times a year. He's a fine fly-caster, so I'll bet he had a pretty smooth golf swing.

As for young Quinn, sometimes he whiffs and sometimes he whales on it, but the sparkle never leaves his eyes. He's been hitting balls since he was three years old, well before his father foolishly embarked upon this quixotic return to the game.

When the little squirt smacks one up on the practice green, his old man exclaims, "Great shot!"

"Dad, I love golf," the kid says.

Oh dear.

Day 398

Item in the club newsletter: Groundskeepers are planting 225 new pine trees around the golf course to enhance "playability."

For whom—squirrels?

Day 400

This morning I hit only two of seven fairways, but I return home to cheerier headlines: Ohio congressman Bob Ney, that thieving suckfish, is pleading guilty to corruption charges in hopes that a judge will show mercy.

One of Ney's many crimes was accepting a free golf trip to Scotland. He and a half-dozen other Republicans played seven courses in five days, including the hallowed Old Course at St. Andrews. The man who picked up the tab—from the chartered Gulfstream to the green fees—was lowlife lobbyist Jack Abramoff, who is also packing for prison.

Abramoff specialized in ripping off Indian tribes that had competing gambling interests, while paying off GOP lawmakers with campaign donations, gourmet meals, skybox tickets, vacations and other goodies. In exchange, the senators and congressmen gave special attention to bills benefiting Abramoff's clients.

Lots of politicians love golf, a weakness that special-interest groups avidly exploit. In 1999, Abramoff accompanied six Republican senators and fifty fellow lobbyists to St. Andrews. A year later he

returned with another golf nut named Tom
DeLay, the future House majority leader
and currently a criminal defendant in
Texas.

Greedy Bob Ney got his invitation from
Abramoff in the summer of 2002. Other
notables on the flight manifest included
Ralph Reed, the former head of the
Christian Coalition, and David Safavian,
then a hotshot in the second Bush
administration.

Golf Digest published a terrific column
by Dave Kindred lambasting this gang for
sullying the historic Old Course with their
loathsome presence. The article featured a
photo of Abramoff, Ney and the other
jerkoffs, posing on the tarmac in front of
their jet. If the judge goes easy on Ney, he
might be out of the hoosegow in time for
the 2009 Pebble Beach Pro-Am.

It's sobering to contemplate how many
bribes have been negotiated in this country
during casual rounds of golf. There ought
to be a law that anytime a politician and a

lobbyist tee off together, the foursome must be rounded out by two FBI agents.

Day 401

Facing a sinister easterly wind, I decide to play Quail Valley's back nine first and get the worst behind me. Unaccountably, I shoot 40, probably the best string I've ever put together.

A wiser person would have called it a day, but vaingloriously I set out to conquer the front side. The script unfolds as expected—three 7s, each more clownish than the last. I finish the round with 88, a numerical barrier that I cannot seem to break.

On balance, I shouldn't bitch. I made several decent golf shots—more, in fact, than I probably deserved.

Although the course was buzzard-free today, I did encounter a red-shouldered hawk feasting on an unrecognizable mammal in the 11th fairway. To avoid

disturbing the regal predator, I politely
snap-hooked my drive into a nest of distant
bunkers.

Day 409

After a week of fishing, I'm back at Quail,
expecting the worst. Amazingly, I shoot 40
on the front nine, and that includes a
couple of idiotic three-putts.

On the difficult par-3 eighth, where I
usually dump at least one tee shot into the
lake, I stick a 6-iron thirty feet from the
flag. What the hell did I eat for breakfast?

On the back side I open with consecutive
pars, so now I'm obliged to keep playing.
Although I'm not striking the ball well, I'm
scrambling like a true grinder. Looming
ahead are the two holes I most fear, the
uphill 17th and bunker-pocked 18th,
which as usual are playing against the
wind. I double-bogey both of them,
another clutch finale.

Nonetheless, the scorecard reads 85,

topping my previous best-ever by three strokes. Just to make sure, I re-do the addition: Eight pars, seven bogeys and three doubles. It occurs to me that I didn't knock a single ball in the water, an aberrancy that's had a salutary effect on my stroke count.

It really is impossible to complain about shooting 85, only thirteen months after returning to golf. I could quit all over again and be happy. In fact, I **should** quit again, before the scabrous claw of doom drags my score back up to the mid-90s and beyond.

I've done what I set out to do—beat the best round from my youth. What else is there to prove?

The smart move is to put away the sticks while I'm feeling warm and fuzzy about the game. Definitely.

Day 412

What a hopeless bonehead I am—straight from the dentist's chair to the first tee, pain-on-pain. Only three days after playing so well, I've developed a scalding shank.

On the 10th fairway, I spook a bald eagle that's been wolfing down the remains of a carp. I misguidedly greet this sighting as some sort of mystic omen—an eagle on the wing portending an eagle on this tricky par-5?

When I slice my next shot into the lake, it becomes clear that the true omen was the dead carp. I close with two doubles and a triple on my way to a 90.

Should've quit when I had the chance. Definitely.

Day 413

Lupica advises me to play the perilous closing holes at Quail Valley over and over until they are my friends. Perhaps then I'll stop gagging down the home stretch.

When I start describing my new world-class shank, he cuts me off and exclaims, "Don't ever use that word!"

"What?"

"That word that begins with 's.' Don't even say it!"

He seems painfully intimate with the affliction.

Day 416

Talk about toxic mojo.

I hook a fairway wood over a hill and nearly take out the only other players on the course, who are teeing off on a parallel hole. Rushing to apologize, I see that the foursome includes my friend Joe Simmens, the very person who'd talked me into giving golf another try. Today he's having second thoughts.

This is only Joe's second visit to Quail Valley, so the odds of meeting him here— much less nearly beaning him—were remote. It's good that I didn't put him in the hospital, since he is also the general contractor on our new house.

The encounter leaves me so flustered that I hit an even wilder tee shot off the next tee. Finally I locate my Titleist 1—or what I presume is my Titleist 1—in nappy turf behind a row of trees. I chip out anemically, and when reapproaching the ball I notice, to my dismay, that it's not mine. I am fairly sure of this because the name "Alan" is imprinted on the side.

Manfully I absorb a two-stroke penalty for striking the wrong ball (USGA Rule 15-3), and record a 7 on the hole. Being in nearly pristine condition, "Alan" becomes my new water ball, performing gallantly until falling victim to another snap-hook on the 11th.

Later, when I tell Leibo how I nearly smoked my builder with a blind 3-wood, he says, "In other words, no one is safe. You're basically the Typhoid Mary of the golf course."

Day 419

A wake-up call at 4 a.m. from my throbbing hip. Once the sun is up, I ride out to Quail Valley with Bill Becker.

Today's numbers are 43–46, including five three-putts. The high point of the round is hitting a 6-iron a yard from the pin on the despised No. 8. The low point is blowing the birdie putt.

Day 436

On the first hole I park my drive in the right rough. There I find my stance impeded by a formidable deposit of raccoon shit. I'm certain of its provenance because, unlike the average golfer, I have raised raccoons and cleaned up after them.

What's the official ruling here—do I get a free drop from animal droppings? Perhaps it depends on the species of critter—no relief from rabbit pellets; two club-lengths from a bear pile. I'm guessing that the issue seldom arises at Augusta.

After a short deliberation, I briskly disperse the coon doo with my 7-iron. I finish the nine at 46, with a self-imposed asterisk.

The Downhill Lie

As soon as I get home, I whip out the USGA Rules of Golf and check the index for "Scat, mammal."

Nothing. Ditto for "feces," "crap," "guano" and "poop."

However, under the term "loose impediments" are listed stones, leaves, twigs, branches, worms, insects and . . . dung!

Because Rule 23-1 plainly states that "any loose impediment may be removed without penalty," chipping the raccoon shit was totally proper and legal. The fact that I'm so pleased to have complied with this regulation is alarming.

Camp Ernie

I probably wouldn't have quit golf in 1973 if I could have snuck out of town and gotten my swing fixed. That's what thousands of struggling hackers do now. For about the same price as a hemorrhoidectomy, you can spend several days at a golf school operated by a world-famous instructor.

Golf instructors become world-famous by coaching pros who win major tournaments and are kind enough to mention them by name on network television. That's what happened to a lucky fellow named David Leadbetter. In 1985 he began working with a promising young English player named Nick Faldo. Two years later, when Faldo won the British Open at Muirfield, he glowingly praised Leadbetter for turning his game around.

Faldo went on to take five more majors, and Leadbetter went on to become a franchise. Over the last two decades he's done for yuppie golf instruction what Hooters did for chicken wings.

Partnered with the sports superagency IMG, Leadbetter now has twenty-six "academies" located around the world, including South Korea, Austria, Portugal, Japan and Malaysia. Among several stateside Leadbetter camps is one in Bradenton, Florida, that offers live-in quarters for junior golfers who split their days between practice and academics.

From across a fairway, Leadbetter in his banded straw hat might be mistaken for Greg Norman, one of his luminary ex-students. And like Norman, Leadbetter has crafted an empire from a golfing persona; his likeness is stamped on shirts, visors, balls, swing training devices, cocktail coasters, headcovers and, appropriately, money clips.

The high-end demographic of Leadbetter's clientele is evident from his brand-name associations with Callaway, Rolex, Cadillac, Jos. A. Bank apparel and Sentient, a corporate-jet-leasing firm. He also writes golf books, pens a column for **Golf Digest** and appears often in a star capacity on the Golf Channel. Among his current pupils are Michelle Wie, Ernie Els, Nick Price, Trevor Immelman and Lee Westwood.

Leadbetter's flagship operation is located at the ChampionsGate resort in Orlando. I made reservations for a four-hour playing lesson ($875), followed by an all-day session on the range and in the video room ($1,750). Such sums must seem asinine to non-golfers, but hard-core players will gladly raid their 401(k)s for the promise of a healed swing.

A Leadbetter clinic is the hacker's equivalent of Lourdes. The private attention of the great man himself is in such demand that, according to **Golf Digest,** he charges $10,000 for an all-day lesson.

Needless to say, I didn't bother to inquire if Leadbetter was available for a private session (he wasn't; he was attending a PGA event in Tampa, keeping a tutorial eye on Mr. Immelman, among others).

My instructor was a likable young guy named Steve Wakulsky, who joined the Leadbetter operation in the early 1990s and worked his way up to Worldwide Director of Training and Certification. For five years Wakulsky ran the Leadbetter facility in Bangkok, which he acknowledged was a pretty sweet gig for a single guy. Now married and the father of two small children, he teaches at the Orlando academy, not far from the relentless wholesomeness of Disney World.

Wakulsky introduced himself while I was hitting some balls, trying to warm up. The first cold front of autumn had swept through central Florida, and the temperature on the practice range was 49 degrees, made colder by gusts up to 25 mph—masochistic golfing conditions, unless you're Scottish.

"It's really windy," Wakulsky said. "Wow."

"Ridiculous," I agreed.

Wakulsky, who is from Michigan, hurried off to find a heavier jacket. Then, bundled like natty sherpas, we headed for the first tee at the Norman-designed ChampionsGate National Course.

Along the way, I gave a quick history of my wobbly relationship with golf. Wakulsky seemed impressed that I'd returned to the sport after so many years, and urged me not to be too self-critical. It was, I explained, an occupational hazard for writers.

When he noted that for the whole front nine we'd be playing into the teeth of the wind, I felt relieved. Here was a sterling excuse for hacking; any rotten shot could—and would—be blamed on onerous gusts.

I began by wafting a tee shot 89 degrees skyward with my 22 degree rescue club. The ball seemed to hang forever at the top of its mortar-like trajectory, then noodled to earth only 125 yards down the fairway. "At least you're in play," Wakulsky remarked after the wind swept his drive deep into the left rough.

We both scrambled for bogeys on the opening hole, then lowered our shoulders and soldiered onward. Because I hit the ball fairly high, there was no evading the northeasterly blow. My shots were swooping and looping so capriciously that I had to laugh, despite the fact that it was the most expensive partial round of golf that I'd ever played.

Wakulsky offered some helpful suggestions, but his primary mission was to observe my basic swing and the multiple variations thereof. The next day, on the range, is where the painstaking task of retooling would take place.

The Downhill Lie

We played slowly. Wakulsky gave pointers on my setup and club choices, and helped me read the greens—there's nothing like a stiff wind to demolish an already tremulous putting stroke. On the front nine I managed three pars along with two bogeys, three doubles and a triple.

The finest part of the morning occurred during a comfort break. Wakulsky pointed at an animal creeping out of the palmettos and said, "What is **that**?"

"A bobcat," I told him.

"Really?" Wakulsky had never before seen one, although the species was once a dominant predator throughout the South.

This uncommonly bold bobcat was attempting to stalk a flock of sandhill cranes, a stately-looking bird with a red featherless crown. Fortunately for the birds, the tawny cat was as obvious on the velvet-green fairway as the proverbial turd in the punchbowl. The cranes eyeballed her immediately, and began bleating like asthmatic goats. After a few minutes the frustrated feline abandoned the hunt and scampered back into the scrub, where her kittens had been waiting for lunch.

Wakulsky and I resumed our march of pain. Once we made the turn and began playing downwind, it seemed reasonable to expect that our shot shaping would improve. His did, but mine got worse—horribly worse.

After I slaughtered the par-5 13th with a series of septic shanks, Wakulsky glanced at his watch and said he had another lesson starting soon back at the academy. We played one more hole and headed for the clubhouse.

"I see a few things we can start on right away tomorrow," he told me. "I think we can do it in a day. It's not like we've got to rebuild your whole swing."

"That's good," I said skeptically.

"You obviously love the game. I can tell," Wakulsky said.

Translation: Why else would you put yourself through such agony?

"There's no problem with your distance," he added. "You should feel good about that."

The Downhill Lie

"Too bad I can't hit it straight."

He said, "You've got too much going on with your lower body."

Well, I thought, there was a time . . .

Then came those words that make every hacker cringe: "You've got a lot of potential. You really do."

"Thanks," I replied, through clenched jaw.

Wakulsky meant well, but not a lesson goes by when a struggling player doesn't hear that he or she has "potential." It begins to sound like charity.

Back at the hotel, I tried to cheer myself with a copy of **Who's Your Caddy?** by Rick Reilly of **Sports Illustrated.** It's a collection of essays about how Reilly conned his way into caddying for famous golfers and celebrities. He is a very entertaining writer, yet I found myself unamused to learn that Donald Trump, who's older than I am, can hammer a golf ball 310 yards. I comforted myself with a petty vision of the cocksure billionaire trying to tee off in 25-knot gusts, his famously surreal hair torqued into cotton candy.

I put down the book and looked out the window of my room. The depressing view explained the presence of a mother bobcat on the busy golf course: She had nowhere else to go.

ChampionsGate is hemmed in by highways and housing subdivisions, a typical panorama of unbound Florida sprawl. Where no rooftops are sprouting, there are barren future homesites—miles of bulldozed flatlands upon which not one green twig remains. The last refuge for the bobcats, sandhill cranes, deer and other critters was the golf resort property with its piney woods, raw palmetto scrub and freshwater lakes.

The same story is unfolding all over the place; as rampant development destroys wetlands and wooded habitats, golf courses become sanctuaries for the displaced wildlife. Occasionally nature bites back with a vengeance. Last year, a rabid otter attacked a female golfer on the seventh hole of a country club in Vero Beach. The woman's companion went after the animal with a long iron, which only fueled its derangement.

The Downhill Lie

After chasing both players from the course, the mad otter scampered into an adjoining subdivision and chomped two other persons before being subdued by wildlife officers.

I was still thinking about my peaceful bobcat sighting as I went downstairs for dinner. Among the five conventions at the resort was an assembly of psychologists, but I steered clear of them at the bar. They were talking golf.

The next day was warmer and not so breezy. Wakulsky set up a video camera and recorded me hitting a 5-iron. Then he positioned me in front of another launch monitor where, unfathomably, I started hitting the ball a mile, straight as a laser beam.

Santiago, the fellow operating the machine, clocked my clubhead speed at 105 mph. He said I should switch to steel shafts. That sort of comment is tonic for the ego, but poison for the mind. Wakulsky mildly suggested that I refrain from splurging on new golf clubs until I acquired a repeatable golf swing.

We went to a screening room to review my technique, which was somewhere between unpolished and ugly. As soon as Wakulsky turned on the tape, I cringed.

My friend Leibo is right when he says there's nothing more uncomfortable than watching video of one's self hitting a golf ball. "It's like seeing your mother naked in the shower," he says. "You have to look away."

Speaking of Mom, she's always been a stickler for good posture. I wish I'd listened to her. On the tape my stance looked round-shouldered and tilted oddly to the left; the swing was loopy and hurried. The effect was that of a vertigo patient, threshing wheat.

Using an electronic stylus, Wakulsky began pointing out all the flaws. My right hand was too far on top of the grip, my weight was in my heels, my shoulders were too far open, my right elbow was folding up, my left wrist was too cuppy, my legs were too busy . . . and, of course, my posture was dreadfully hunched.

"Your whole upper body looks more like a

turtle shell," Wakulsky observed, helpfully drawing a curved line along my profile.

To further illustrate the problem, he froze my setup position on the right side of the screen. On the left side he inserted, in the same pose, none other than Ernie Els.

Using a famous pro as a split-frame model is common in modern golf instruction. It's probably not intended to leave a student feeling hopeless and emasculated, but the risk is large.

Els has one of the silkiest swings in the world; mine is better grooved to whacking rodents. Watching us side-by-side on video, one would require an agile imagination to figure out that we both were playing the same game.

Nonetheless, I suppose it's helpful to know that my downswing descends on a 61 degree plane, while Ernie typically uncorks at 58 degrees. That sort of thing can be fixed; the disparities in our age, size and muscle mass cannot.

If the technology had existed three decades

ago, I might have been curious to see myself on a wide television, swinging in tandem with Jack or Arnie. But now, being on the proverbial back nine of life, the gap between excellence and what is possible seems insurmountable. It's like studying a John Holmes video before making love to your wife—who're you trying to kid?

Back on the driving range, Wakulsky placed me between some fruit-colored Styrofoam noodles and set about "tweaking." Our main mission, he said, was to shorten my backswing and train the wrists to cock sooner, à la Els. That's not how Tiger Woods takes back a golf club, but I'd be elated to make even a pale version of Ernie's swing.

Wakulsky armed me with a baton-like device that had round magnets attached to the shaft. The magnets were designed to slide, clicking together smartly on a properly executed backswing and follow-through. Before long, I sounded like a one-man festival of castanets.

Steve seemed authentically encouraged.

The Downhill Lie

He reclaimed the baton, dropped a ball in front of me and presented a 6-iron. As I took my stance, a swarm of new swing thoughts buzzed like hornets inside my skull:

> **Left arm straight.**
> **Right hand under.**
> **Tilt your body to the right.**
> **Chest up.**
> **Tailbone out.**
> **Left hip higher.**
> **Head over the ball.**
> **Break the wrists.**
> **Touch your right shoulder with the club on your follow-through.**

Here's what I know about the middle-aged brain: It doesn't hold nearly enough information, and what it does hold leaks like a worm-eaten dinghy.

"Your head will explode," Leibo had warned me before the lesson, and he knew what he was talking about.

Every speck of advice that Wakulsky had

given was solid, but if I tried to checklist every point on every golf swing, it would take eight bloody hours to finish a round. Standing over the ball was a paralytic experience; I felt tight, twisted and off-balance. Worse, the shots I was hitting were neither pretty, nor straight.

Yet, watching the new swing in the screening room, my setup and backswing looked a thousand times better. I looked, in fact, like an actual golfer.

"It's still you," Wakulsky said. "It's just a better you."

Deepak himself couldn't have put it better. I was still slicing the ball, but, by God, my posture was superb.

Flipping to split-screen, Wakulsky pasted my old swing up on the left side (in Ernie's spot) and my new swing on the right.

"Night and day," he declared, adding, "It's probably better-looking than it feels right now."

No argument there. The new swing was about as comfortable as bowel cramps. Wakulsky assured me that I'd get used to it.

The Downhill Lie

Off we went to the putting green, where he placed eight balls twenty feet from one of the holes. I sank four in a row before he even got the camera warmed up. It was ludicrous.

"I couldn't do that again in a hundred years," I said unnecessarily, and proceeded to pull the next three dozen putts.

As a kid, I'd used a blade putter that allowed me to switch from right-handed to left-handed on a whim. Wakulsky said he didn't recommend that system, and instead proposed that I stand farther away from the ball and stop breaking my wrists.

We finished with bunker shots and green-side chips, Wakulsky providing a few simple tips that produced immediate results. I allowed myself to feel guardedly optimistic.

After a final video recap, Wakulsky burned a DVD of Ernie and me so that I could study it at home. He said that I had the ability to be a good golfer, that I shouldn't let myself get discouraged, and that I definitely shouldn't quit the game again.

I thanked him for his help, and then

selected my complimentary David Leadbetter cap, shirt and lesson book.

On the trip home, one thing that Steve
had said stuck in my mind:

"You want this game to be fun."

Sure, I want this game to be fun.

I also want peace in the Middle East, a
first-round draft pick for the Miami Dol-
phins and a lifetime of reliable erections.

Wanting, however, won't necessarily make
it happen.

Day 444

On my first day back from the Leadbetter
Academy I am sideswiped by the most
dreaded disorder in golf—a shank.
Aborting my round on the eighth hole, I
hurry to the range, where the condition
proceeds to worsen with each swing.

After fifteen minutes I give up in despair.
For the first time since I started golfing
again, I am seriously considering heaving
my bag into a canal.

The Downhill Lie

Everything I know about shanks is black doom. There are several theories about how a golf ball comes to be impacted by the stem of a club's shaft—the hosel—instead of the face of the blade. Whatever the cause might be, the result is sickeningly unmistakable: The shot flares radically to the right.

Worse, shanking is like the hiccups; once you start, you never know when you'll stop.

Many players are so fearful of the shank that they refuse to utter the word. Harvey Penick, the fabled golf teacher, preferred to call it the "Lateral Shot."

The shank is to hackers what the clap is to porn stars. Unfortunately, penicillin won't cure a shank. The condition abates only when the gods of golf take mercy on your soul, so from now on all references to it will be masked with dashes.

Day 446

My first full eighteen in almost four weeks, again in a blustery wind. I complete the first hole without a single sh_ _ _, so I'm practically euphoric despite the triple-bogey.

The highlight of the front nine is a curling twenty-footer to save bogey on the fourth. On the back side I'm in the water twice, and for good measure stack on a couple of listless three-putts.

But, for once, I finish with minor heroics and a smile. After my worst drive of the afternoon—possibly of the year—on the lengthy and difficult 18th, I rally from the boonies by scorching my rescue club about two hundred yards. Then I pitch a wedge to within six feet and drop the putt for a par.

The final damage is 93. If I'd scored that high after shelling out $10,000 for a private day with David Leadbetter, I'd probably be homicidal. Now I figure I got off easy.

Later, Mom calls and asks, "How's the golf going?"

"It's hard to say."

"Aren't you finding it at least a little relaxing?"

"It's not relaxing, Mom. It's a diversion," I say. "There's a difference."

"Diversions are good, too," she says.

"That's true."

"Even if you can't relax."

"It's just the way I am."

"I know, son," Mom says fondly. "I know."

Day 448

A friend and biologist, Derke Snodgrass, tells of a recent adventure in Senegal, where surly monitor lizards kept mistaking his golf balls for stork eggs and snatching them off the fairways.

If the PGA had any imagination, it would release large, aggressive reptiles during all major tournaments. Talk about boosting the ratings! Who wouldn't tune in to see Phil Mickelson wrestle a Burmese python in Rae's Creek at Augusta, or Vijay

Singh jump a komodo dragon on the island green at Sawgrass?

Day 451

A late nine holes with Leibo, Lupica and Al Simmens, who are all in jolly form. Meanwhile I'm playing as if I've never touched a golf club before.

It's the perfect time to test my new RadarGolf system. Each ball comes equipped with a microchip that transmits its location to a handheld receiver. The closer you get to a lost ball, the louder the receiver beeps.

According to the infomercial, Radar Balls send out a signal up to a hundred feet. In my case, a hundred yards would be more useful.

I tee one up on the fourth hole, enduring a fusillade of mockery from my friends. Every Radar Ball features the image of a hunting dog on point, yet nobody seems to think this is particularly clever.

The Downhill Lie

When my drive obligingly disappears over a hill, I feel a misplaced rush of anticipation. As Lupica and I speed toward the area where the Radar Ball exited the fairway, I activate the receiver, which starts beeping frenetically. That's because five other Radar Balls are stowed in my golf bag, and I've neglected to secure them in the factory-provided satchel, which is specially insulated to block the homing signals.

As a result, the ball-detector gizmo is now tweeting louder than the smoke detector in Willie Nelson's tour bus. Leibo shouts something crude in our direction, but I can't hear him over the noise.

Cresting the hill, I'm dismayed to find my Radar Ball in plain view near the eighth tee—there's no need to track it electronically.

Lupica orders me to turn off the frigging receiver. "This is so embarrassing," he mutters.

I dash down the slope and whack my ball in the imagined direction of the pin.

"Did you see where it went?" I ask.

"No, I did not," Lupica says.

"Perfect!"

At greenside, three balls lie within ten yards of each other on the fringe. I bound from the cart, point the handheld unit and follow the beeps straight to my ball.

"See, it works!" I exclaim, provoking a fresh wave of derision.

Leibo asks how much the RadarGolf kit cost.

"Two hundred bucks," I tell him.

The consensus is that I've been ripped off. Leibo warns me not to bring the gizmo to the Member-Guest tournament because we might be disqualified, or possibly assaulted by our opponents.

"Just wait," I say. "Someday Tiger'll be using these."

Finally, on the ninth, I sh_ _ _ a beauty out of bounds, into some heavy vines along the shore of a lake. Unfortunately, it's not one of the microchip-equipped Radar Balls that's gone MIA. It's a brand-new Pro V1, which I'd teed up by mistake.

Another four bucks down the crapper.

Day 453

Election Day. Golf is rained out, but Bill Becker stops by for a field demonstration of Radar Balls.

He lobs one into a neighbor's yard and we advance as meticulously as prospectors, sweeping the receiver back and forth. It doesn't make a chirp until we're twelve feet from our target, which is sitting up smartly and quite visible on a tuft of sod.

A glaucomic Pomeranian could find a ball at a distance of twelve feet, which is exactly eighty-eight feet shy of the advertised range of the patented RadarGolf homing device.

Bill says a refund is in order. I say the golf industry shamelessly traffics in false hope. First the Q-Link, now the Radar Balls . . . even a sucker like me gets wise after a while.

Day 467

America's most despised casual golfer, O. J. Simpson, is making headlines again. A New York publisher has scotched a book in which Simpson re-creates the stabbing murders of his former wife and a male friend, crimes for which he was famously acquitted.

The tome was to be titled **If I Did It,** to which informed readers might have replied: What does he mean "if"?

Simpson was said to reimagine the vicious attacks through a hypothetical character named "Charlie," and editor Judith Regan had breathlessly promoted the book as a virtual confession.

Its release was to be timed with prime-time interviews on Fox TV, but the public reacted to the hype with such gastric revulsion that even cold-blooded media baron Rupert Murdoch (who owns both Fox and HarperCollins, the publishing company) was compelled to kill the project days before the big launch.

The Downhill Lie

Characteristically, Simpson is shrugging off the fiasco. Today he told a Miami radio interviewer that he's already spent the book advance, a high six-figure sum that he sensitively described as "blood money." Meanwhile, the families of Nicole Brown Simpson and Ronald Goldman are still awaiting the $33.5 million that a civil jury ordered Simpson to pay.

The ex–football star insists that **If I Did It** was not a confession, and that he didn't murder anybody.

So now he can resume his lonely but intrepid quest, searching every golf course in South Florida for the real killers.

Day 468

As if we needed more proof that golf is a pandemic disease, today a Russian cosmonaut used a gold-plated 6-iron to hit a ball off the International Space Station.

It wasn't a scientific experiment but rather an exorbitant commercial stunt. A

Canadian golf equipment manufacturer, Element 21, paid the Russian space agency an undisclosed sum to stage the shot, which was filmed for use in future advertising.

Unfortunately, the swing thoughts of cosmonaut Mikhail Tyurin were agitated by a kink in a cooling hose that caused his space suit to overheat before he could line up the shot.

"Oh rats," grumbled Tyurin, upon withdrawing to an airlocked chamber for repairs.

More than an hour later he tried again, this time laboring in his weightlessness to achieve a proper stance over the ball. At one point he was actually floating upside down, a sensation not unfamiliar to gravity-bound golfers.

Eventually the Russian was able to hold steady long enough to make a one-handed swing. The ball—weighing only three grams, and unapproved by the USGA— departed with a pronounced slice into the cosmic void. The script allowed for a mulligan, but the frustrated cosmonaut called it quits.

A spokesman for Element 21 boasted that Tyurin's shot will travel for billions of miles and circle the earth for years—a typical golfing lie. NASA engineers calculate that the ball will orbit for two or three days before dropping into the atmosphere and burning up.

We should all live long enough to see a slice go up in flames.

Day 474

Tomorrow begins the Florida leg of the book tour for **Nature Girl,** a new novel of mine. I'll be accompanied by Paul Bogaards, a vice president of the publishing company, who's coming not to chaperone so much as to escape the current inclemency of the Northeast.

A boisterous golfer, Bogie has booked tee times at several tough courses along our route, and I'm already a mental wreck just thinking about it. He's a much better player than I am, and the fact we carry comparable handicaps is a testament to the inscrutable rating system employed by the USGA.

To prepare, I've scheduled a lesson at Quail Valley with our unflappable Director of Golf, Steve Archer, who is familiar with my multiple swing glitches and free-floating neuroses.

I'm on the way out the door when the phone rings. Bad news: The only paved road to the course has been closed for emergency repairs by the Department of Transportation. The lone alternate route is a long dirt road, which, it turns out, has been transformed by heavy rains into a muddy roller coaster. A few cars have gotten stuck, and several others have turned back.

In my case, retreat is not an option. This is my last chance to pick up my clubs for the road trip.

The Downhill Lie

Soon I'm skidding through a spitstorm of bile-colored mud. Fishtailing in front of me are two battered, enormous dump trucks, one of which offers a warning in crude block letters on its tailgate: UNINSURED.

I struggle to keep a safe distance from the trucks, which isn't easy in the absence of traction. At such moments I feel no guilt whatsoever about piloting an SUV. If I was in a Prius, I'd need a snorkel.

Twenty minutes later, I arrive at Quail Valley, where I'm greeted with stares of incredulity in the pro shop. No other golfers have made it to the course since the road was shut.

"How did you get here?" Archer asks.

"Four-wheel drive," I say.

He laughs. "You still want your lesson?"

We spend an hour on the range in a cool drizzle. Then I stow the clubs in my splattered ride and plow back down the highway of mud.

Master of Disaster

A common golfing myth is that the more frequently you play, the better you'll get. Often the opposite is true, as anyone who lays off for even two or three weeks can attest. Over a seven-day road trip I was facing five rounds, all at unfamiliar courses. Bubbling with optimism I was not.

Bogie flew in from Newark and met me in Orlando, where he'd booked us at a Marriott that advertised, among other amenities, a Nick Faldo golf school. Coincidentally (or perhaps not), it was located very near the ChampionsGate facility operated by the teacher whom Faldo had made famous, David Leadbetter. I wondered if Nick, too, got $10,000 for a personal lesson. Having won so many tournaments, he could probably charge more.

However, Bogie and I were avoiding all

instruction. The morning after my first book signing, we drove to a course called Grande Pines. There he announced that we'd be playing from the green tees, just one box short of the dreaded tips. Surreptitiously I previewed the scorecard, which listed a sobering Slope Rating of 135 and a distance of 6,612 yards.

Trouble commenced immediately, a flurry of three-putts and triple-bogeys. Before we reached the third tee, I'd lost two balls and Bogie had lost four. A vocal and exuberant competitor, he made no effort to suppress his disgust.

The fellow who'd been assigned to play with us, a taciturn radiologist we shall call Doc, seemed entertained by my companion's purple eruptions. Doc was a good player and a nice guy, offering yardage readings from a handheld range finder. The way I was swinging, it didn't help much.

While probing the underbrush for one of my errant drives, Bogie let out a cry and nimbly bounded away from what he claimed was a "huge" snake. It turned out to be a harmless black racer no more than three feet long, evidently a monster by New Jersey standards.

On another hole, I rescued a large slider that was crossing a dirt road used by utility trucks. While I was carrying the turtle to a safe location, it ungratefully peed all over my golf shoes, a fitting commentary on the day.

The course had been laid out to accommodate one of those typically charmless golf developments, boxy condominium buildings extruding within easy range of my banana slice or Bogie's towering hook. On a couple of occasions it seemed certain that one of us had sent a flier into somebody's boudoir, but there were no telltale sounds of breaking glass or human moans.

I believe it was the fourth or fifth tee where Bogie pointed down the fairway and made a sour yet profound announcement: "There ought to be a rule that you can't put a golf course within sight of a theme park."

There, rising forty stories in perfect line with the flagstick, was a garishly painted spire called the Sky Tower. It's the main visual landmark of Sea World, home of Shamu the Killer Whale and other trained sea mammals. Visitors ascend the Sky Tower in elevator capsules that, according to the attraction's Web site, offer a grand view of "downtown Orlando"—the highlight of any vacation, to be sure.

On the same day Bogie and I played Grande Pines, a killer whale at the San Diego Sea World got mad at his trainer and twice dragged him to the bottom of the tank, fracturing the man's foot. No such drama broke out at the Florida theme park, where eagle-eyed tourists high in the Sky Tower had to settle for the sight of a middle-aged fool mangling a nearby golf course.

Bogie rallied for a 90, while I heroically parred the final hole for a 101. Trees were the problem. There aren't that many at my home course, which has been shredded by recent hurricanes. If you miss a fairway at Quail Valley, you're usually in the drink, the gnarly rough or a stand of saplings—but never, ever lost in a forest.

As the name implied, Grande Pines was **muy grande** with pines, not to mention palmettos and oaks. By the end of the round, the combined tally of lost balls was eleven—six for me, and five for Bogie. Our golf bags were noticeably lighter when we loaded them in the car.

Two days later, a Saturday morning, we were staring down the wooded maw of the impressive opening hole of Copperhead, at the Innisbrook resort north of Tampa. The course was packed, carts lined up at the first tee like buses at the Port Authority in Manhattan.

It was my first round on a course that hosted a regular PGA event, the Chrysler Championship, which K. J. Choi had won a few weeks earlier with a score of 13-under. Choi had made brilliant use of his driver, but mine would be staying in the bag. To minimize misadventures off the tee, I'd decided to borrow a page from Tiger's playbook and stick with the 3-wood.

Bogie had been heavily lobbying to play

from the tips, the same as the pros, but I told him to forget it.

"Okay, we'll go from the golds," he said.

The scorecard showed 6,725 yards. It promised to be a long, **long** day.

We were paired with a sturdy-looking couple from Oslo, Norway, who were characteristically polite and quiet. They flinched but did not complain whenever Bogie bellowed the f-word, which happened on more than one occasion. In a way I felt sorry for him, now outnumbered three-to-one by tight-lipped Scandinavians.

He and I both started ignominiously, posting 7s on the same dogleg par-5 that Choi had eagled on the final day of the Chrysler. My ball visited three different bunkers, all superbly groomed, before landing anywhere close to the green.

The second hole was equally comical, Bogie and I racking up another nasty pair of 7s. The Norwegians played briskly and with purpose, spending little time mulling club selections or studying putts. We picked up our pace, so as not to be left in their dust.

On the front nine, a rare triumph: Bogie and I parred the hole known as "Snake Bite," a long par-3 that had inflicted upon Choi his only double-bogey of the tournament.

Bogie made the turn at 49, while I shot 47 with three pars. I wasn't totally displeased, but I feared the wheels would soon fly off—and did they ever. I debauched the back nine with three 7s and three 6s, on the way to a 53 and the malodorous sum of 100. My lag putting was so inept that at times Bogie seemed dumbstruck.

Only once were the Norwegians rattled, and not by us. Copperhead is home to a bizarre species of squirrel that looks like a cross between a howler monkey and a fox with thyroid problems. Agile and crafty, the squirrels specialize in preying upon unwary golfers by stealing snacks and slurping from unattended beverages. It was behind the 14th green where the Norwegians encountered one of the pointy-eared beasts looting their cart. They frightened it away with their only emotional outcry of the day.

Despite being terrified of the squirrels, Bogie played revoltingly well on the home stretch, finishing with a 42 that could easily have been a 39. As was his custom, he kept the scorecard to himself until we were in the car, when my hands were on the wheel and free of sharp lunch utensils. He endeavored to put a positive spin on my sorry performance.

"It's better than you did last time," he said.

"By one fucking stroke," I pointed out.

"Hey, it's a tough course."

"Paul, for me they're **all** tough courses."

The next morning found us somewhere east of the Sarasota airport, hunting for the Ritz-Carlton Members Club. It turned out to be a stunning tract bordered by a nature preserve—and not a condo in sight. In fact, the clubhouse hadn't even been finished.

A gloss of dew was still on the grass when Brian and Frank, our caddies, led us to the first tee. We were the only human souls on the course, which felt eerie but liberating after the traffic jams at Copperhead and Grande Pines.

Frank advised us to be cautious searching the woodlands for our wayward balls, due to a robust population of rattlesnakes. There were also wild boars, Brian added, fully tusked and disinclined to give ground. Bogie said we should make a pact not to venture off the fairways.

He was flying back to Jersey that afternoon and, because the following day was his birthday, I agreed to play from the tips. Even though the distance was intimidating (7,033 yards), I vowed to remain upbeat.

Like Quail Valley, the Members Club is a Tom Fazio design, which means man-made elevation, deep lakes and a plague of sprawling sand traps. I told myself that nearly a year of playing Quail Valley had prepared me for another Fazio challenge. Besides, an experienced caddy would be helping me pick my clubs and read the greens. Theoretically, there seemed no reason not to score better.

The Downhill Lie

Again, I failed to factor in the most corrosive fundamental of golf, the Suck Factor. On any given Sunday, any course can be butchered.

The final damage was 105, the worst number I'd posted since buying my clubs. Even with Brian at my shoulder, I was putting like a caffeinated chimpanzee. The round included an especially macabre stretch of three three-putts, followed by a triplet of hard-earned 7s. Even Bogie ran out of encouragement.

Inexplicably, amid the carnage I managed to par the two longest holes on the course. Another sunny interlude occurred on the 15th, when I hit a rescue club 210 yards off a trampled ridge between two bunkers dotted with fresh tracks of feral pigs. The ball poinged over the green, but it was still an awfully crisp shot.

That I had not destroyed my Callaways by the end of the morning was, I felt, a sign of growing maturity. The hike itself had been glorious under a porcelain sky teeming with birds—cranes, wood storks, ospreys, curlews, swallows, blue herons and red-tailed hawks.

There are worse places to play bad golf than on the edge of a wild cypress swamp.

After surrendering the scorecard for my review, Bogie left to catch his flight home. I was bitterly amused to see that, having miscounted my flails on the 16th, he'd given me 104 instead of 105. Dourly I corrected the mistake, which I hoped was not a deliberate act of pity.

With the Member-Guest tournament at Quail Valley only thirteen weeks, five days and eleven hours away, I phoned Leibo to warn him of my decline. He absorbed the news extremely well, probably because he'd shot 73 that afternoon.

It seemed impossible that only a few weeks earlier I'd been scoring in the low 90s—and bitching about it! Now I would happily trade places with Scooter Libby, just to break 100.

The gruesome gauntlet resumed at the melodramatically named Black Course at Tiburon (Slope: 138), a Greg Norman project in Naples. Playing alone, I made exactly one decent swing all day: a choked-down

5-iron from a waste bunker, uphill into a mean wind. The ball landed eight feet from the pin, but I squandered the opportunity by clumsily stubbing the putt.

At one point I found myself trapped in a construction site roaring with backhoes and bulldozers. A wide roadbed was being laid through the back nine, undoubtedly to accommodate future high-end homesites. It was an offensive but commonplace Florida scene—greed on the roll, a tide of concrete and asphalt where once there were tall pines and creeks.

A forklift operator eventually noticed me wheeling the golf cart in circles, and he hoisted an immense water pipe to clear a path to the next tee. By now, the din and dust from the earth-movers had pulverized the wispy remnants of my concentration. Queasy from diesel fumes, I hooked the next drive into a mesh-lined borrow pit, and sullenly moved on.

By the time I departed Tiburon, the state of my demoralization was complete and seemingly irreversible. I'd missed sixteen of eighteen greens, posting only two pars on the way to another rancid 100. The most exhilarating moment came when I almost flipped the cart while speeding along a boardwalk toward the 17th tee.

Back at the hotel, I began scheming cowardly ways to bail out of finishing the golf book. One possibility was to schedule another operation on my right knee, which would put me on crutches long enough to blow my publisher's deadline. The only drawback to that plan was my profound aversion to pain—rehabbing a knee joint is no fun.

The following morning, I got up early and drove to Miami to appear on a live television program. The segment preceding mine featured a peppy performance by the cast of **Altar Boyz,** an off-Broadway musical about a Christian boy band. It was a challenging act for a novelist to follow.

Afterwards I headed to the Lago Mar Country Club in Plantation, not far from where I grew up. I was filling out a foursome with Al

The Downhill Lie

Simmens; Tommy McDavitt, another old friend; and Al's stepson, Patrick, a nice kid and a sharp golfer. To make me feel better about my own erratic play, Patrick recalled that he'd once shot 109 a week after posting 76.

The story did cheer me up. The only reason I couldn't top it was that I've never come close to shooting a 76.

When Al, Tommy and I were kids, the Lago Mar area of Broward County was the boonies, a vast and almost impenetrable stand of melaleuca trees. A papery-barked species that sucks water like a giant soda straw, melaleucas had been imported from Australia to drain the Everglades for development—a mission that flopped.

Many thousands of acres of native flora were displaced by the exotic pests, which wreaked mayhem on the ecosystem. The trees proved so durable and prolific that the state of Florida has spent hundreds of thousands of dollars trying to eradicate them using helicopters that squirt potent herbicides.

The developers of the Lago Mar golf community came up with a localized solution to the melaleuca epidemic: They bulldozed an immense clearing in the trees. Hanging in the clubhouse was an old black-and-white photograph that showed a canal where I once fished for bass. If the waterway still existed, it was now irrigating acres of suburban backyards.

Despite the bittersweet memories, the round at Lago Mar was therapeutic. It's hard to embarrass one's self while playing golf with guys you've known since childhood. I couldn't make sense of all the betting, which was just as well. I carded a 91 and Al had an 81, and somehow we collected $28 from Tommy and Patrick. More importantly, I broke 100 for the first time in a long, demeaning week. The relief was indescribable, and a bit pathetic.

After being brutalized in swift order by Grande Pines, Copperhead, the Ritz Members and Tiburon, Lago was a pardoning intermission. Afterwards I felt ready to go home and be punished by a familiar golf course.

The Downhill Lie

I missed Quail Valley's turtles, the mutant carp and even the savage 18th hole.

And, of course, there was a tournament to prepare for.

Day 484

A jolting and unforeseen complication:

"Guess what I'm doing next Wednesday," my wife says.

"What?"

"Having my first golf lesson."

"Really?" Me, thinking: **Easy now. This will pass.**

Day 488

A Christmas card arrives from the David Leadbetter Golf Academy: Santa Claus wearing a golf glove and sunglasses. He's carrying a bagful of swing aids and other clubhouse goodies bearing the Leadbetter brand. Call me Scrooge, but the greeting fails to put me in the holiday spirit.

Meanwhile, Fenia is seeking fashion advice for her upcoming lesson. I tell her to dress comfortably.

The skirt she chooses is cute, although she'll have to be careful when teeing up the ball.

As for footwear, I advise her to wear sneakers. She is reluctant, because she doesn't want tan lines on her ankles.

"They won't let you wear flip-flops," I say.

"How come?"

"They just won't."

Day 489

Today's the day—my wife's first lesson. Afterwards she calls from the car to say she had a grand time, which catches me off guard.

"I was using a pitching wedge," she reports proudly.

"That's great. It's very important around the greens."

The Downhill Lie

"What's a green?" she says.

Me, thinking: **One step at a time.**

"Did you schedule another lesson?" I ask.

"Not yet. It's kind of expensive."

I hear myself saying, "You should do it again, if you enjoyed it."

"It was fun!"

After Fenia says goodbye, I immediately phone Lupica for advice. He can hardly stop laughing.

"She liked it?"

"Apparently so," I say.

"This is the greatest," he cackles. "I was just thinking: How many different ways can golf screw you?"

Although I love spending time with Fenia, Lupica's right—the golf course can be dangerous territory for a marriage. The last thing a struggling hacker needs is a spouse who wants to learn the game, and the last thing a beginner needs is advice from a spouse who's a struggling hacker. Delicacy and reserve—not my strong suits—will be necessary to ensure that the conjugal relationship survives our relationship with golf.

Sensing that my days of solitude at Quail Valley are numbered, I head straight to the club and tee off—alone—under overcast skies. During the round I soak five balls, but on the upside I one-putt four consecutive greens, a personal best. The final damage is 93, which, after my calamitous road trip, shimmers like a gem.

Day 491

Baffling but true: After posting those four humiliating triple-digit scores from the book tour, I watch my USGA handicap rise a measly one-tenth of a stroke, to 15 even. Einstein couldn't unravel this tangled formula.

Day 497

Delroy Smith is back in town after a season of caddying at Burning Tree, the premier power-golf venue in Washington, D.C. I'm hoping for tales of dissolute congressmen galloping naked with their bimbos on the fairways, but Delroy says the summer was routine.

His eyebrows hitch when I tell him I've signed up for the Member-Guest Invitational.

"Okay," he says, "this is important for the tournament: Always make sure you know which holes you're stroking on."

"Stroking" is one of those terms that has come to mean something entirely different in middle age than it did when I was young.

"I'm still not sure how that works," I admit.

"Say your handicap is eighteen—is it eighteen or fifteen?"

"Eighteen on this course."

"Okay, let's say you're playing a guy who's a nine. That means you get a stroke on nine of the holes."

I stare as if he's speaking Slovenian.

Delroy patiently takes out the scorecard and pencils an asterisk below the holes that are handicapped 1 through 9, in descending degrees of difficulty. I'd just parred the first hole, which—because I was "stroking"—would count as a birdie in a match.

The system, which is actually quite simple, rewards average players who play well on the hardest holes. Unfortunately, I customarily save my double- and triple-bogeys for the easiest holes, which in competition would nullify the benefits of stroking.

Although it's mid-December, the temperature in central Florida is 79 degrees and a hard wind blows from the southeast. The greens at Quail Valley are so dry and fast that every downhill putt becomes a runaway train. I limp home after another body blow to the handicap.

"We're peaking at the same time," Leibo

quips when I check in. "Remember when I was a five? Now I'm a seven, with a bullet."

When I gripe about the pace of the greens, he chuckles. "As bad as they were today, I promise you they'll be worse for the tournament. Same with the pin placements."

A survivor of many club tournaments, Leibo tells me to prepare for the "pucker factor," referring to the nervous and involuntary constriction of a certain orifice.

The puckering, I assure him, has already commenced.

Day 498

An improbable scene: My wife in the backyard swinging the Fred Funk–endorsed Momentus Training Club.

"This thing really is heavy," she comments.

"Forty ounces," I say. "That's why it did a number on those rats."

Fenia frowns in disgust. "**This** is what you used on the rats?"

She shoves the Momentus into my hands. Practice is over.

Earlier, she and young Quinn each had a golf lesson.

"Dad, I hit a bird!" Quinn announced excitedly when he got home. "But don't worry, it flew away."

"How did you hit a bird?"

"I don't know. The ball went really high."

My wife confirms the incident. Her own lesson, she reports, was uneventful.

Day 503

Fenia and I head out to practice, a trip fraught with volcanic risk. Following the stern counsel of experienced golfers, I keep my mouth zipped until my wife shows an interest in my advice, which on occasion she does.

The Downhill Lie

For clubs she's using loaners that are too long, although she doesn't complain. She whiffs a few balls, tops a few and yet remains undiscouraged; in fact, she acts like she's having a blast. Such a healthy attitude seems eerily out of place on a driving range.

Afterwards, at Fenia's urging, we try a short par-3, her first-ever complete hole of golf. She's so stoked that we play another. On the way home, we stop at a golf store and she picks out shoes—but only one pair, an act of retail restraint that I accept as a small miracle.

My friends are of two views regarding spouses who take up golf. One faction thinks it's very cool, while the other believes it's Shakespearean tragedy.

"Unacceptable," David Feherty weighs in by e-mail. "As they say in Spanish, 'Feliz Nueva Anus!' "

Which he translates loosely to mean, "Congratulations on your new orifice."

Day 508

New Year's resolutions:

    1. Improve my short game.
    2. Find an antacid that works.

Lupica's got his whole family scouting magazines and catalogues for lame golf gimmicks that I can purchase under the guise of "research." Son Zack has triumphantly unearthed an advertisement for Visiball sunglasses, which supposedly filter out greenish hues so that you can locate missing balls in deep rough or heavy woods.

According to the manufacturer, "Visiball glasses are equipped with a specially designed lens that blocks out the majority of the foliage and grass from your field of view when you are looking for your lost golf ball. With the foliage and grass out of the picture, your lost golf ball stands out like a sore thumb."

The product carries an intriguing warning: "Visiball lenses are NOT golfing sunglasses. In fact they are not meant to be worn while playing. They are designed to be worn only when searching for a golf ball."

This could be a hot item on the South Beach party scene.

At $40, the X-ray-like shades look like a bargain compared to the expensive and disappointing RadarGolf system. However, the online demonstration of Visiball is lame. The "missing" golf balls are conspicuous in the Before picture, and only slightly more so using the special blue-tinted lens.

"I'm not falling for this one," I tell Lupica.

Day 509

After a week of diligently practicing chips, bumps and lobs, I disgrace myself around the greens. Two positive notes: I'm suddenly driving the ball well and also executing decent bunker shots.

These trends are, like all progress in golf, ephemeral. At this point I couldn't make the Flomax Tour.

Day 513

On my wife's birthday, the entire clan descends on Quail Valley's par-3 layout. There are only six holes, but—because Fenia is new to the game, and Quinn has short, first-grader legs—it takes us an hour and a half to finish.

Still, everybody's cheery and content, walking in the sun. We're like the flipping von Trapp family, minus the harmonies.

Day 514

Candid appraisal from Jack, another veteran caddy at Quail: "You can play, you just can't score."

Which is better, I suppose, than

being told that you can't score **and** you can't play.

Day 516 / Key West

From an African-American juggler performing at Mallory Square:

"Hey, folks, what do you call 150 white guys chasin' a black guy?"

Crowd: "What?"

"The PGA tour."

Day 519

The seventh fairway is lousy with jumbo-sized crows—hundreds of the raucous pests, clotting the trees and blackening the rough, cawing, "Ugh-uh, ugh-uh, ugh-uh."

They're right, too. I get mired in a bunker and double the hole. It's a Hitchcock moment, the crows scoffing as I flee toward the next tee.

Day 523

We're slogging along the front nine when Delroy spots a young bald eagle wheeling over one of the lakes. The bird banks to the north and alights beside its mother in the top of an oak, where it poses with spread wings and fanned tail.

"Two of them! I wish I had my camera," Delroy says.

"When you're fishing, eagles are always good luck," I tell him, and smoothly par the next two holes.

No sooner are we out of sight of the birds than I double-bogey the 10th.

Delroy remains a stalwart envoy of positive thought. "You're getting better, much better," he says. "I know where you came from, pro. Remember the first time I caddied for you?"

"Yeah, but I still can't score."

"That'll come. It will."

In an unbelievable stroke of good

fortune, Delroy has consented to caddy for me and Leibo during the upcoming Member-Guest. It's a major coup, because Delroy usually caddies for the very top golfers, including the current club champion (age seventeen).

"I've been working hard on my short game," I assure him.

"You're doing the right thing," he says diplomatically.

Two more pars, a nasty trio of 6s, then I scramble home with a pair of hard-won (and welcome) bogeys.

Walking off the 18th green, where I'd improbably landed a 6-iron on the upper tier, Delroy smiles and says, "I'm impressed."

"That was fun," I hear myself say.

The f-word? On a golf course?

Despite skulling five wedge shots (including one that flew forty yards out of bounds), it was sort of fun.

As my kids would say, how sick is that?

Day 524

In Fenia's presence, I boldly carry a demo putter to the practice green. She is surprisingly open-minded.

"Why don't you buy it, if you like it?" she asks.

Today she's being fitted for her first set of clubs. Possibly this accounts for her libertarian mood.

It's now official: My wife is taking up golf. The decision has potentially seismic implications for our union, not to mention my handicap.

Another comforting e-mail from Feherty: "You're doomed."

Day 525

I'm not good enough for you.

That's what I murmur to the Cameron putter that had been a gift from Fenia. Discreetly I lean it in the back of my locker, next to the banished blue Ping.

The Downhill Lie

I've fallen for a fresh new face, the one with which I openly dallied on the practice green. It's a TaylorMade Daytona Rossa CGB, an offset model with a 3.5 degree loft and a headweight of 335 grams. I have postponed breaking the news to my spouse.

According to TaylorMade, the Rossa has twelve anti-skid grooves and a "Titallium insert" designed for "exceptional forgiveness on mis-hits."

I have no idea what Titallium is, or exactly where it's been implanted into the head of the putter. I am, however, painfully familiar with the concept of a mishit. The promise of exceptional forgiveness holds great appeal.

The deal goes down in a dark corner of the pro shop. Rossa isn't as sleek or as elegant as the Cameron, but her raspberry grille and shiny tungsten plugs exude a brash, saucy attitude.

She certainly livens up my bag.

Day 526

Titallium sounds like it should appear near titanium (Ti) in the Periodic Table of Elements, but there isn't a trace of it anywhere on the chart.

Research reveals that no such substance occurs in nature; Titallium was formulated by the TaylorMade company explicitly for insertion into putters. A Google expedition confirms the fact.

"Maybe it's like kryptonite," Leibo muses.

Personally, I don't care if it's a freaking gum wrapper, as long as it helps me sink a few putts.

Meanwhile, Peter Gethers, my editor, phones for a book update. I inform him that, despite hours of practice, my game isn't improving; in fact, there's been steady erosion in the scoring department.

"I haven't broken 90 in three months," I admit.

"Really?" Peter means to sound sympathetic, but he doesn't fool me for a second.

"The prevailing view," I say heavily, "is that the worse I'm playing, the better it is for the book."

"Yes," Peter says, "that's the tragedy of this entire undertaking, isn't it?"

Day 528

It might be true love.

Playing for the first time with Rossa, I make five pars and a birdie—and commit only one three-putt, which was entirely, totally, completely my own damn fault. Not Rossa's.

I would've broken 90 handily if it weren't for three triple-bogeys, which offset my putting heroics. Next time I'll try not to let Rossa down.

Day 531

She's a goddess—on the first hole I drain a twenty-five-footer to save par. Can't hit a driver or a wedge to save my soul, but all day long Rossa valiantly carries the load.

Because of the unusually warm, dry winter, a fish kill has occurred at Quail Valley. The skies and shorelines are once again dark with hungry turkey buzzards, which squabble with the resident eagles over rotting carp carcasses. Neither Delroy nor I is clear about whether the USGA considers dead fish to be "loose impediments," so on No. 14 I end up chipping—successfully—from a crispy hash of scales and bird-pecked bones.

I would have carded an 89 except for a penalty stroke on the 18th green: The ball, which lay in some fluffy fringe, moved a half-turn as I squared the putter behind it.

Again, not Rossa's fault.

Day 533

A new experiment on the practice range: Teeing the ball with my left hand.

This was suggested by Steve Wakulsky,

The Downhill Lie

my instructor from the Leadbetter Academy, responding to a plaintive e-mail in which I'd laid out the symptoms of Exploding Brain Syndrome, or EBS.

Wakulsky agreed that I overstuff my skull with golf tips. "Obviously the analytical left side of your brain is too attached to your swing," he said. "You freeze over the ball because you are using the left side of the brain to swing your club."

Because right-handers are dominated by the left hemisphere of the brain, Wakulsky said, teeing the ball with the left hand should activate the right (and more creative) hemisphere, triggering a freer, calmer swing.

While conceding that the theory "might sound a bit wacky," Wakulsky said it has helped some golfers overcome EBS.

And initially it seems to work for me, which is a bit scary. The drives that I hit after teeing up left-handed definitely seem straighter and longer than the others.

I might also be hallucinating, which is a whole different problem.

Day 535

"It was a fun day."

The f-word, from Tiger himself, after winning his seventh consecutive PGA tournament with a ho-hum 66 at the Buick Invitational. He is now 124 strokes under par for his last twenty-eight rounds of PGA golf.

Over a comparable stretch, I am approximately 560 over par. Maybe I should try teeing up with my tongue.

Day 538

It's no easy feat to hit ten fairways in regulation and still shoot 97. I could blame the weather (45 degrees at tee time), but the sad truth is that saucy Rossa and I are quarreling on the greens. The spat included a dismal string of three-putts.

The Downhill Lie

What happened to the mystical powers of Titallium? I wonder. And where is Rossa's "exceptional forgiveness"?

The rest of my short game is a wreck, too, despite all the practice. On the third hole, a seventy-yard bunker shot soars far beyond the hole and over a hill, where it strikes the foot of a woman on the practice green near the clubhouse. She is unhurt, and sympathetic to my plight.

Although the Member-Guest tournament is only six weeks away, Leibo insists he's not worried.

"I don't want to embarrass you out there," I say.

"You can't embarrass me. It's not possible," he says. "I don't care if you show up wearing nothing but—" and here he describes a lewd ensemble that features, among other things, two strategically placed jingle bells.

"Remember," Leibo says, "our mission is to have f-u-n."

Enough with that word.

Emerald Pity

I was comfortable playing golf exclusively at Quail Valley. As treacherous as the course could be, it was familiar—like an irascible but occasionally softhearted drill sergeant. At Quail I had butchered every hole and also parred every hole, so there were few surprises; no bunkers I hadn't dimpled, no lakes I hadn't bombed, no trees I hadn't clipped. Each hazard was an old acquaintance.

Nothing inspiring ever happened when I took my shaky game to another course. On strange fairways, my swing defects became magnified; on strange greens, my putting stroke turned gelatinous.

So I was perfectly content to stay at Quail and flail away in peace, by myself. Lupica wouldn't hear of it. He said that I was missing out on some great experiences, that no golfer could appreciate the glory of the sport without exploring new venues.

"Another couple years, I'll be ready," I said.

"See, that's what I'm talking about. You've got a very poor attitude."

As it happened, Lupica was coming to Florida to cover the Super Bowl for the **Daily News.** He insisted that I make plans to meet him at a club in West Palm Beach called Emerald Dunes, another celebrated Tom Fazio design. Formerly one of the top public courses in the nation, it had been purchased and made private by a group including John Haas and Frank Chirkinian, the former sultan of CBS Sports.

Among other achievements in broadcasting, Chirkinian revolutionized the way television covers professional golf. Today the cups on all greens are painted white because Chirkinian figured out that white cups made the holes more visible to TV viewers—and to the golfers. The use of videotape, crane-mounted cameras and blimp shots were all Chirkinian innovations. It was none other than he who started the now universal practice of listing players' scores in strokes over and under par.

Known at CBS as "the Ayatollah," Chirkinian reigns with imperiously gruff affection over Emerald Dunes, and his stories (some fabulously unprintable) were worth the visit.

But I played execrably—couldn't chip, couldn't putt, couldn't pull it together and break 100. Worse, I was lousy company for my partners. Lupica's friend, Henk Hartong, christened me "Eeyore" because of all my bellyaching.

Upon returning home, I announced for about the nineteenth time that I was considering re-quitting the game. My wife listened patiently, said all the right things and then went back to chopping the salad.

I walked to my office to read the news on the Internet. Judging from the headlines, lots of people in the world had had a much worse day than I did. In Baghdad, 130 innocent men, women and children had been blown to bits by a car bomb; their offense was to be Shiite Muslims, shopping in a public market. Closer to home, near the central Florida town of Deland, search teams had pulled the twentieth body from the matchstick rubble left by a series of hellish tornados. Among the dead was a boy of only seven, the same age as my youngest.

Reading about those tragedies, I felt small and corrupted with self-absorption. Short of cardiac arrest (or a poisonous tick bite), nothing of mortal significance is likely to occur while one is whacking a small dimpled sphere across gentle green grass under a warm tropical sun. Only a miserably manic soul—and I'm not alone—would allow such a pleasantly inconsequential distraction as golf to be ruined by a scorecard.

Yet every weekend, thousands of otherwise rational men and women are cursing, kicking at divots and smashing expensive milled putters against the trunks of immovable hardwood trees. These players go home in a toxic funk to inflict gloom upon their loved ones until the following Saturday, when they rush back to the golf course and do it all over again.

Trying to be good at something isn't a bad idea. But, in the turbulent and random scroll of life, topping a tee shot is a meaningless if not downright comic occurrence. A few players I know appreciate this truth; they shrug off their flubs and placidly move along. Such inner peace is as enviable as it is elusive.

My goal in golf was to attain a modest level of proficiency. Put another way: I didn't want to play like a total putz. That's not asking for the moon, but, on days such as this, the dream seemed slippery and faraway indeed.

Becoming a decent player certainly requires dedication, but letting one's self morph into a profane and volatile depressive is unsound, not to mention unappealing. I definitely needed to get a grip.

Over the phone, Leibo cheered me with a restorative anecdote about a mutual friend, Tony Rudolph, who that afternoon had launched a 3-wood a distance of minus three yards.

The Downhill Lie

The circus shot was all the more incredible because Tony was hitting off a pristine lie in the middle of the fairway. "I don't know how he did it," Leibo said, "but he swung down and hit the ball dead into the ground. It bounced straight up in the air, with backspin."

They used a handheld range finder to verify what they'd witnessed with their own eyes. Initially Tony's ball was 204 yards from the hole; after he bludgeoned it, the new yardage measured precisely 207 on the same line.

"We were crying," Leibo said, "we were laughing so hard."

Of all my butt-ugly golf shots, I had yet to hit one backwards.

So there was that to be grateful for, too.

Day 543

Overheard at a local sporting goods store, from a man slightly older than me, being fitted for new clubs: "Tiger Woods and I are exactly the same height."

And we should give a rat's ass because . . . ?

Day 544

After only two weeks, Rossa, the tramp, betrays me.

I sink a thirty-foot teaser for a bird on No. 2, but then it's all downhill . . . and uphill and sidehill, including a memorable four-putt meltdown on No. 5.

Afterwards, Quinn accompanies me to the practice green for an informal father-son contest. He's got his pint-sized blade, and I've retrieved the Scotty Cameron from time-out in my locker.

Rossa? She is dead to me now.

Day 548

I consult with Bill Becker about how best to dispose of the scarlet harlot. "I don't believe in the destruction of equipment," he says, "but I do believe in watery graves."

"The lake?"

"Absolutely. You have to put it someplace

where there's no chance that you two can ever get back together."

"The putter's in my locker," I say.

"You've gotta get it out of there," Bill advises sternly. "The 10th green is perfect."

He's right: Water on all sides.

Yet, upon arriving at the golf course, I cannot bring myself to send Rossa to sleep with the fishes. I ignore her as I remove my golf shoes from the locker.

Today I have a nine-hole playing lesson, in which I hope to display my odious short game for Steve Archer's professional appraisal. On the first hole we both hit nice drives that roll to a stop near a very large alligator, sunning by the lake.

"That's the biggest one I've ever seen out here," says Steve.

It's at least eight feet long; maybe nine. A real tank.

Gators are common on Florida golf courses, providing a mobile dimension to the concept of "lateral hazard." The largest ones are the most fearless; they are remarkably swift on land, and have a brain the size of a Brussels sprout.

But in my twisted world, the sight of a ravenous territorial reptile that outweighs a golf cart can only be a positive omen. Sure enough, I start striking the ball better than I have in weeks.

It's not until the fifth hole that I finally sh_ _ _ a pitching wedge. Then, on No. 6, I uncork a 9-iron on a flight path like that of an Iranian RPG.

Being the savvy instructor that he is, Steve promptly repairs both my swing and my head. On No. 7 I stick a 9-iron eight feet from the cup. Although I miss the birdie, I cruise home feeling that it's a tolerable pastime, this golf.

Day 549

My good-luck gator is still lurking near the first fairway, and I'm hoping he sticks around until the Member-Guest tournament. Under his cold stare I par the hole, then scramble onward to an 88. Scotty Cameron and I are homies again— I three-putt only two greens, and drain a couple of timely ten-footers along the way.

The only flat note: I dunk three consecutive drives into the water on No. 3, terrorizing a flock of ducks that have come to Florida to escape winter. The bombarded fowl fly off in a frenzy, reorganize at a safe altitude and vector due north.

Even iced, Lake Erie must be looking pretty good.

Day 550

A low-pressure system rumbled through overnight—I put the exact time as 3:30 a.m., because that's when my knee and hip began to play dueling bongos. My grandmother wasn't making up stories when she said she could track barometer fluctations by the pain in her arthritic joints.

Day 552

After weeks of loyalty, the Cobra driver forsakes me in a cold wind. Still, I recover often enough with a borrowed 56 degree Vokey wedge that I decide to order one from the pro shop.

If nothing else but for mojo maintenance, I ought to have at least one Titleist club in my Titleist carry bag.

Day 556

It's too chilly for practice, so I stay home and thumb through golf books, another rookie mistake.

On page 117 of **Ben Hogan's Five Lessons** is an illustration indicating the "correct location of calluses" on a golfer's left palm. Hogan's diagram shows eight calluses, but my hand has only seven—and the one on my ring finger appears to be slightly off the mark.

To a stickler like Hogan such details

were important. Most golfers would never think of counting, much less mapping, their calluses.

I call Al Simmens to tell him I've only got seven.

"That's it," he says with a laugh. "Your game is done."

Big Al has never added up his calluses, and he expresses a high degree of skepticism about the inquiry. By way of advice, he says, "Number one: Stop reading these books."

I track down Leibo, who was deranged enough to play a tournament in today's arctic blast. He reports having only one callus on his left hand.

"Hogan says you're supposed to have eight," I tell him.

Leibo sighs. "I hate golf and I don't want to talk about it anymore."

I locate Lupica by cell phone in Boston.

"Did Hogan wear a golf glove?" I ask.

"No! Why do you think I don't wear one?" Lupica says. "He was my hero."

I confide to having only seven of the eight requisite calluses.

"The Missing Callus," he muses. "It could be a **Da Vinci Code** sort of mystery."

"But I wear a glove, so why do I have any calluses at all?"

"Maybe you're squeezing the club too tight. Hey, you know what else? Hogan had an extra cleat on one of his golf shoes!"

"You're kidding."

"I don't remember which shoe. He ordered them specially from London, I think."

That figures.

Day 558

After making a nice par, I hear high praise from Delroy: "Walk tall, pro."

Then I fall steadily to pieces over the remaining holes. With only seventeen days until the tournament, my game continues a hellbound descent. The more hours I spend practicing, the worse I seem to get, a demoralizing correlation that flies in the face of universal golf wisdom.

The orthopedist can't see me for three weeks, which kills my last-ditch scheme of scoring a medical excuse to bail out of the Member-Guest.

Day 560

There are more enjoyable ways to pull a groin muscle than by schlepping one's own golf bag, but this is what I deserve for slicing so many shots into impassable locations.

After eight holes I gimp back to the clubhouse, then head home in hopes of spousal sympathy. My wife regards my injury with the clinical detachment of a combat nurse, and to my dismay prescribes only rest.

Day 561

I have a semi-encouraging conversation with a fellow named Jack Chapman, who gave up golf for twenty-five years and later returned to the sport with some success. The difference between Jack and myself is that he was a scratch player when he mothballed his clubs, while at the time of my retirement I was mauling par. Stellar genetics are another factor: Jack's father, Dick Chapman, was an extraordinary amateur golfer who won the 1940 U.S. Amateur Championship, the 1951 British Amateur and during his long career played in nineteen Masters tournaments, tying Charlie Coe for the amateur record.

Jack and I are watching the Accenture Match Play Championship on television. Uncharacteristically, Tiger Woods is wildly pushing his tee shots into lakes, cactus patches and other hazards. Except for their extreme distance, his drives look creepily like my own.

At one point Tiger is down four holes to Nick O'Hern, but magnificently battles back to square the match. Then, on the first playoff hole, he misses a four-foot birdie putt—an unexpected sight that Jack and I can hardly absorb. Tiger drops the match and snaps his winning streak of seven consecutive PGA tournaments, raising the possibility that he might, after all, be mortal.

Day 562

Emergency lesson with Steve Archer.

The mission: To confront a virulent new case of the sh_ _ _ _ _, The Swing Disorder That Must Not Be Mentioned By Name.

We play nine holes, and although I par the last three in a row, the sh_ _ _ manifests itself often enough that Steve is visibly alarmed. By late afternoon he's got me chipping short wedge shots using only my right hand. "You need to do a lot of this," he says. "I mean a lot."

In addition to the sh_ _ _ _ _ and some weak lag putting, the third most distressing thing we witness on the course is a mangy seagull stripping a fish from the talons of a bald eagle—our majestic national bird, being mugged by the avian equivalent of a garbage rat.

Rotten-bad mojo.

I feel lucky to make it back to the clubhouse.

Day 564

A farce at Lago Mar, beginning on the first hole where I dunk two balls. The sh_ _ _ _ have set in so stubbornly that Big Al refuses to watch me hit any irons, fearing that through some funky osmosis he, too, will be infected.

The round is notable for the most ridiculous bogey that I've ever made; that possibly anyone in the history of golf has ever made. It occurs on the par-5 13th, where I:

(1) Hook my drive to the soggy bank of a drainage canal;

(2) Sh_ _ _ an 8-iron back across the fairway and over two small hills;

The Downhill Lie

(3) Sh_ _ _ a 6-iron into another fairway, where the ball comes to rest beneath a tree;

(4) Bump a low 9-iron into a grassy mound, which redirects the ball toward a wooden footbridge upon which it bounces not once but twice before landing improbably on the green;

(5) Where I come within a half-turn of sinking the downhill thirty-footer for par.

At one point during the carnage, Leibo shows up to check on my progress. He has spent the morning undergoing a nuclear stress test, which he would have failed if he'd been wired up while watching me flail with a wedge. It's been an inauspicious debut for the new 56 degree Vokey.

After only a few holes, Leibo excuses himself, saying he has an important meeting with his tax accountant. This might be true, or it might be a polite fiction. In any case, he's not there to observe my clutch finish, three-putting the 16th, 17th and 18th holes.

The tournament is eleven days away, and my game's in the proverbial shitter. I call my book editor, and recount the day in gruesome detail.

"Hmmmm. It sounds like things are getting ugly," Peter says, with a hint of hopefulness.

No Such Luck

Boat captains in the Florida Keys won't let you bring a yellow banana aboard because it brings bad luck. This is a known fact.

Believing is everything, and I believe mojo is real. If I get skunked on two consecutive days during a fishing tournament, my hat goes into the nearest garbage can. If that doesn't bring back some positive karma, I'll switch brands of candy bars, forsaking my regular Skors for a Milky Way (always bring two, sometimes three; never just one). And if **that** doesn't work, I'll substitute a baked ham sandwich—or, if extreme measures are necessary, roast beef—for my customary turkey sub.

This behavior is every bit as twitchy as it sounds, yet it produces results. What you eat, what you wear, even what you put on your head are all proven factors in a day's sporting fortunes. Example: I own four particular T-shirts that consistently bring good luck on the water. Frayed and faded, they're juiced with such heavy mojo that I'll use them until they tatter to lint. Conversely, if I suffer an exceptionally bad day of fishing in a brand-new shirt, it will be consigned to the rag bin.

Upon returning to golf I was pleased to learn that many players are as superstitious as fishermen. PGA pros often carry sentimental items for luck—Jim Furyk keeps his golf shoes in a tote bag from the University of Arizona, his alma mater; Lorena Ochoa marks her ball with a coin engraved with her favorite prayer from the Old Testament. Some pros use only balls bearing a certain numeral, while others avoid specific numbers as unlucky; David Toms, for instance, refuses to hit a No. 2 ball off the first tee.

Even Tiger Woods has his rituals—he uses head covers knitted by his mother, and he always wears red on Sundays. Tiger could easily afford to discard his shirt after a crummy round, or even after a crummy shot, but most amateurs can't.

No matter how poorly I've scored, I still haven't tossed any $80 Cutter and Bucks in the Dumpster at the end of a day. During rocky stretches I've switched hats, tees, ball markers, gloves, bandannas, spikes and even sunglasses, but high-end wardrobe I cannot bring myself to jettison. Unlike my fishing clothes, golf duds aren't cheap. Another factor is marital harmony—because many of my shirts were presents from my wife, I'm reluctant to start throwing them away on an impulse for fear of being branded as ungrateful and possibly nuts.

As the weekend of the Member-Guest drew closer, I hurried to tidy up my karmic mess. I sorted through my stash of designated water balls, purging the most scrofulous. I consigned to a closet several hats that had let me down during the finishing holes of potentially respectable rounds.

Finally, I removed from my golf bag a medallion featuring the creepy visage of a hairy, bloated Irish troll. A gift from Leibo, the tag came from Whistling Straits, a sadistically demanding course in Kohler, Wisconsin. Leibo had half-jokingly warned that the souvenir (which resembled a leprechaun who'd been dipping into Barry Bonds's private vitamin jar) might possibly be an agent of bad mojo—and, in fact, my game had been sputtering ever since he'd given it to me. I unclipped the medallion and stowed it safely out of sight.

As for good-luck charms, I owned none. It had been so long since my last semi-decent round of golf that the accoutrements from that day had lost their magic, or were lost themselves. The quarter that I'd used to mark my putts was either in a soda machine or

Quinn's piggy bank, while the Titleists that had performed so ably now slept with the carp at Quail Valley, or lay plugged deep in snake-infested flora.

Hope arrived one February afternoon when, on the way to the Keys, I stopped to visit my mother. As we were chatting in the kitchen, I noticed a small plastic bag on the table. The bag was old and brittle-looking, bearing the logo of a local jewelry shop.

"What's this?" I asked her.

"Dad's watch. I was wondering if you wanted it."

In the bag was a handsome but simple wristwatch that I recognized right away. It has a gold-and-steel band, and the back is etched with my father's initials, K.O.H.

The watch is visible in a framed photograph of Dad standing beside a large blue marlin that he caught in the Bahamas. It's the same watch he was wearing on the night he'd collapsed and died at home. Mom had kept it all these years.

Once someone broke into the house and

stole most of the family jewelry, which wasn't much but included some irreplaceable heirlooms. Although the thief found Dad's wristwatch, he didn't take it. When my mother got home she spotted it on top of the dresser, where the intruder had left it.

We all wondered why he'd swiped everything but the watch, which was worth about $1,500. Police detectives told Mom that professional burglars avoid items that are engraved, because they're hard to fence. The explanation sounded plausible, although I was aware of many cases in which the crooks were not so cautious.

For whatever reason, my father's watch had survived the ransacking.

"I thought it might be nice for you to have," Mom said, "though I know you like the one you've got." She leaned closer to check out mine, an old stainless Submariner with a faded black face.

"This is the one Dad gave me for Christmas," I reminded her, "just before he died."

She seemed surprised, and touched. "And you're still wearing it after all this time?"

"Yup."

She smiled and squeezed my hand, which always gets to me.

"I'd like to have this one, too," I said, "if you're sure."

"Lately I've been going through all his things—"

"I'll keep it, Mom. Maybe someday I can give it to Scottie or Quinn."

"It still works," she said.

I slipped off my watch and put on my father's, which was a bit loose on my left wrist. A jeweler could make it snug by removing a link or two from the band.

"Looks good on you," said Mom.

"I'll wear it," I promised, and placed the watch back in the plastic bag. I was thinking about the upcoming tournament—if anything might bring me good luck on a golf course, it would be carrying something personal that had belonged to my Dad.

And if that didn't work, so what? Wearing the watch would make me think of him, which couldn't be bad.

After dinner I said goodbye to Mom and drove down to Islamorada. The next two days were filled with some of the best tarpon fishing I'd experienced in a long time. Upon returning to Vero Beach I immediately took Dad's watch to a shop and got the band adjusted.

After thirty-one years it was strange to see a different timepiece on my arm, but it had the weight of major mojo. I locked it in a safe until the day of the tournament.

Day 566

Leibo calls up singing, "Shanks for the Memories."

It's no joking matter, as he will see for himself during the tournament.

"All I need from you is two pars every nine holes," he says. "Two pars, okay? You can sh_ _ _ it all day long and I don't care as long as you give me two pars."

"That's more pressure," I mutter.

"You fucker! I'm trying to take the pressure off!"

"I know, Mike. I know."

Day 568

By e-mail the USGA delivers word that my handicap index now stands at 16.1, which converts to 19 strokes at Quail Valley—a new high, just in time for the tournament.

I've been told that some golfers are secretly pleased if their handicaps spike before a major competition; that a few actually conspire to that goal, submitting higher-than-typical scores with the aim of sandbagging their team into an easier flight.

Silly me. I've been trying to play better, not worse.

Every day at practice, I feel like a

drowning man. Then I come home and see the snapshots of my father that are pinned to the corkboard. I pay special attention to the photo in which Dad is splashing cleanly out of a bunker, a skill that I've recently mislaid. In another picture, he's beginning a downswing with what appears to be a 9-iron, and displaying a textbook rotation of the shoulders. With a form like that, there's no way to sh_ _ _ a golf ball.

No way.

Day 570

The whole clan goes to the range, where the mighty Quinn dominates with his driver, and his commentary.

"Did you see that shot, Dad?"

Then: "Hey, did you see that one?"

Then: "Dad, look at this! Look at this!"

Then: "I love golf. It is the greatest sport."

Quinn's ebullience draws the notice of several older players. Some look amused and some look suspicious, as if I've overdosed the kid on Flintstones vitamins.

We relocate to the practice green. Fenia doesn't have a putter, so I slyly fetch the exiled Rossa from my locker. They bond instantly.

I feel like Oprah.

Day 572

Another dubious achievement: I hit twelve of fourteen fairways, yet post just one measly par. This requires creative ineptitude with the irons.

On No. 11 I clobber a freakishly long drive, 298 yards as paced off from the nearest sprinkler head. From there I strike what looks like a perfectly adequate sand wedge. The ball lands softly in the center of the green and proceeds to roll . . . and roll . . . and then roll some more. It comes to rest off the putting surface in a sidehill cut of fringe, from where I make bogey.

Even my lone par is a fluke—a forty-foot lag on No. 6.

The Downhill Lie

Seventy-two hours until the tournament, and I'm flopping like a gigged frog.

Day 573

One last lesson before match play, and the results are inconclusive.

Steve Archer says the accursed sh_ _ _ _ are the result of sliding rather than pivoting away from the ball. He theorizes that I'm doing this because the pain in my right knee makes it uncomfortable to rotate the hips.

Unfortunately, there's no time to get an artificial joint implanted. Tomorrow is the official practice round.

Strokes of Fate

The practice day of the 2007 Men's Invitational Member-Guest began with a Mind Drive capsule and flashing blue lights: A cop pulled me over, in front of the gates of the country club.

He clocked me at 59 mph, and it would have been faster if I hadn't been stuck behind an eighteen-wheeler. The officer was very decent about it, letting me off with a warning.

"Have a good day of golfing," he said, which is not usually how my traffic stops are resolved. It seemed to be a good sign.

Sure enough, Leibo dropped a fifteen-foot birdie on the first hole. I thought we were off and running, but we were just plain off.

On No. 4 I topped my drive down to the ladies' tee box, banged a 3-wood up near the green, then chunked an easy pitch. Our partners, whom we will (to protect the innocent) call Tom and Tim, were solid players—long off the tee, steady with their irons, and very quiet. Leibo said we were lucky they weren't in our flight. "We'd be getting smoked," he whispered.

My putting was unimpressive, yet on the front nine I delivered my promised two pars, including a swell up-and-down on No. 6. On the back side I parred two more holes, and it should have been three.

On No. 14, a downwind par-5, Delroy urged me to go for the green with my second shot: "No holdin' back, mon." With his range finder he shot the distance to the pin at 208 yards. I creamed the 22 degree rescue club, but the ball caught a front-side bunker on the fly. There I got a chance to display my unspeakably hapless sand game, and ended up with a sad bogey.

On No. 16, the elevated two-hundred-yard par-3, I banged a 5-iron about twenty-five feet past the cup, then three-putted for another wasted opportunity. Leibo did the same—one of six exasperating three-putts for him. Usually a wizard with the blade, he seemed vexed by Quail Valley's slick greens. "It's like putting on the top of my head," he muttered, tapping his shiny dome.

He finished with an 84, and I had a 93—hardly a banner day, but still a personal milestone: the first time I'd played a full round in the company of two total strangers.

No physical violence, equipment abuse or glaring breaches of etiquette had occurred. Not once had I struck my ball out of turn, tromped on a competitor's putting line or spit during somebody's backswing. Leibo said that I might easily have been mistaken for a real golfer.

Afterwards, at the kickoff cocktail party, team pairings were handed out. Leibo and I were in the "Masked Bobwhite Quail" flight, based on an assigned combined handicap of 21—a number that we never quite figured out, even after a couple of cocktails.

Tournament handicaps were based on 90 percent of a player's normal handicap, with a differential of no more than 10 strokes between teammates. Mike's USGA index of 5.8 converted at Quail Valley to 7, which was reduced by 90 percent and rounded down to 6. Add the maximum 10 strokes and my handicap as his partner should have been 16, 3 below my Course Rating.

For some reason I'd been listed at 15, a discrepancy that I dismissed as insignificant;

even with a higher combined handicap of 22, our team would have been slotted in the same flight. Leibo, a wily veteran of best-ball events, tried to explain that the shorting of even a single stroke could potentially cost us several points during the tournament.

A more confident player might have raised the issue with the authorities, but in my brittle mental state the last thing I wanted was another distraction. It seemed fanciful to imagine the final outcome boiling down to a razor-thin handicap disparity. For me, the mere completion of forty-five competitive holes without incident or intervention would rate as a triumph of sorts.

Eventually Leibo and I gave up trying to decipher our handicap status, and turned to the gambling festivities. He said it would be poor form not to bet on ourselves, no matter how astronomical the odds, so we put down $30 in the name of team spirit, and threw another $200 into the flight pool. I also made side bets on two teams in the top flight, each of which had a scratch player.

When the wagering slacked off, the entertainment portion of the program began. The club had hired not one but two stand-up comedians to face ninety-six tired, hungry, thirsty golfers—a brutal gig, even with an open bar.

Leibo and I slipped out shortly after the second comic took the microphone; the guy might have been uproariously clever, for all I know, but what could be funnier than the prospect of two days of tournament golf when you have no short game whatsoever? That was the real joke, and I was my own punch line.

That night, after re-reading some philosophical passages from Dr. Bob Rotella, I finally drifted off to sleep. Serenity and self-confidence did not embrace me. By 2 a.m. I was wide-awake again, tossing restlessly and tormented by flashbacks of sh_ _ _ _ _ wedges.

Fishing tournaments were nerve-wracking, too, but nothing like this. In the backwaters you have the comfort of sequestration; there's but one angler to a skiff, and you can put as much geography as desired between you and your rivals. The isolation removes all risk of being humiliated in front of your peers; a sloppy cast with a flyrod is likely to be witnessed only by you and your guide, who might or might not offer commentary.

In a golf match, though, players compete side by side. Civilities must be maintained; certain events acknowledged. An opponent's good shot requires a sincere-sounding congratulation, while a flub becomes a shared yet politely unmentioned experience. There's no privacy in tournament golf, no tidewater refuge from embarrassment or shame; only naked and undeniable reality, as evidenced by the location of your ball.

Every time I closed my eyes I saw myself banana-slicing a drive into the big lake on No. 9. In desperation I took half an Ambien, which turned out not to be a brilliant move. When the alarm beeped at 6:30, I was a zombie.

In the shower I let hot water drum on my

sore hip for five minutes. Then I gulped an Aleve and a Centrum, and put on my father's wristwatch. Leibo noticed as soon as he got in the car, and asked why I hadn't worn it on the previous day.

"I didn't want to waste any good mojo on a practice round," I explained.

Leibick nodded. "Good idea."

This time we made it to the golf course with no interference from law enforcement. A sign near the practice green announced the putting speed on the Stimp Meter at 12.0, which is slightly slower than a .45 caliber bullet.

Lining up for the breakfast buffet, I realized that I'd again misplaced my focus-inducing Mind Drive capsules, which Leibo found amusing. After a short search I spied one on the carpet near my locker, wiped it clean and downed it with a glass of orange juice.

The first of the day's three nine-hole matches started on No. 14, a reachable par-5 when the wind is favorable. However, the morning was dead calm and I was swinging like a stoned circus bear. The first two competitive golf shots of my adult life dribbled harmlessly along the fairway, and I was out of the hole by the time the others reached the green.

Our opponents, whom we will call Dick and Dave to preserve their privacy, revealed themselves as solid hitters and keen-eyed putters. Quickly they went up 2–zip. "We got 'em right where we want 'em," Leibo cracked, but I couldn't relax.

The scoring was straightforward: Best ball won the hole and one point; in the case of a tie, each team received a half-point. Another point was awarded for winning the match.

Because of my handicap rating, I would be "stroking" on four of the nine holes, which meant a bogey was as good as a par, a par was as good as a birdie, and a birdie was as good as an eagle. The objective is to capitalize on such opportunities, but whenever I was stroking, I was choking.

On our fourth hole, I missed a three-footer that would have won a whole point. The putt wasn't exceptionally difficult, but I stood over the ball with rubbery arms for what felt like slow-motion eternity—and then I pulled it.

Not exactly grace under pressure.

On the very next hole, I drained a thirty-footer that turned out to be meaningless, and on the hole after that I twice knocked my ball in the water. It was a shambling gagfest.

Leibo picked up the slack as best he could, but Dick and Dave were unflappable, save for one glorious moment. We were down 5–2 with two holes remaining when Leibo dumped his tee shot in a collection area on a sneaky uphill par-3. I sh_____ my 6-iron into a distant stand of dense, spiky cover that Delroy implored me to avoid, on account of snakes. I found my Titleist (unplayable, of course) and snatched it out of the vines.

Trudging toward the green, I was surprised to see Leibo with a putter in his hand. His ball lay at the bottom of a grassy slope, at least seventy feet from the cup. I'd figured he would try a lob and hope to hold it on the glassy green, which sloped away dramatically.

Putting from such a scruffy, faraway lie seemed dicey, but Leibo knew what he was doing. The ball trundled up the hill, coasted down the crest, kissed the stick and dropped for a bird. It was a beautiful thing to see.

Leibo grinned. I clapped. Delroy let out a cheer.

Dick and Dave were stunned, but gracious.

The magic didn't last. We demolished the next hole and dropped the match 7–3. By way of a summary, Leibo said, "We played that nine like a couple of ax murderers."

He was charitable to employ the collective pronoun. It was I who had murdered our chances, failing to scrape out a single par. Not one. **Nada.**

Under the circumstances, though, my composure was exemplary—I didn't cuss, shriek, howl, sob, gnash, froth at the mouth, throw any clubs, break any clubs or feloniously insert any clubs. No matter how poorly I was striking the ball, I marched the course with a grim and unflinching stoicism that would have made my Norwegian forefathers proud. I behaved as a true gentleman golfer, which isn't easy when one is playing like a spavined troglodyte.

The second death march of the day began on No. 3, a treacherous, bunker-pocked par-5 with a formidable carry over a broad lake. Our new adversaries were, for the purposes of this account, Jimmy and Joe, big bombers who hydrated themselves with one beer per hole. Joe puffed cigars, wore knickers and smacked the ball a country mile; later we found out that his team had won this tournament three years earlier.

I started off wretchedly, plowing my drive into the water. I struck the second one well, then killed a 3-wood to the front of the green. I was lying four and still very much in the hole, which we ended up halving. Delroy grinned and said, "There's still a lot of golf to play. Anything can happen."

The Downhill Lie

Gradually, I started swinging better and even saved us a half-point here and there. On the sixth hole Leibo gutted another birdie putt, turned to me and winked. "Game on," he said.

The match was dead even when we approached the final hole, a 165-yard par-3 over water. The infamous "Gale Valley" wind had kicked up perniciously, and the flagstick was tucked far back on the green. Delroy said the shot was playing at least 185.

Some sort of heavy mojo was in the air. From the tee I could see one of the bald eagles, hunkered over a fish at the edge of the lake. On the opposite shore was my good-luck gator, snoozing in the sunshine. I glanced down at my wrist and sentimentally tapped the face of Dad's watch.

Delroy handed me the 4-iron, a weapon that in my possession produces a startling variety of flight patterns. For once I hit it both high and straight, the ball stopping eighteen feet from the flag. A momentary silence enveloped the tee box; nobody, least of all me, seemed able to absorb what they'd seen.

It was Delroy who finally said, in typical understatement, "That was the right club, captain."

Walking toward the green, Leibo reminded me that I was stroking on the hole; a par was a birdie. Then he added, "You're gonna hate me for saying this, but it's the truth: The hardest thing to do in golf is try to two-putt for a win, just cozy it up to the hole. But that's what I want you to do, okay?"

The hardest thing in golf? Is that all?

"I wish you hadn't told me that," I said.

The other team wasn't in bad shape; Jimmy had skied one into the lake, but Joe's ball was on the back fringe, no more than twenty feet away. He stroked a superb putt that barely missed on the low side, and we gave him the par.

I did a convincing imitation of a Lamaze patient while Delroy, a genius at reading greens, studied my line. "Right edge," he said. "It's downhill but into the wind. Play it like a flat putt."

A flat putt for a flatliner. Perfect.

Teetering over the ball, I felt fuzzy. I tried to visualize the ideal path and speed, but what appeared in my mind's eye was the image of my Titleist speeding away crazily, like a raindrop sliding down a windowpane.

I held my breath and struck the ball.

My aim was true, but I didn't give the damn thing enough gas. It dicd three feet from the cup. When I glanced anxiously at Leibo, he shrugged—no gimme, but safe. He had a ten-footer for birdie, and I was confident that he'd bury it and get me off the hook.

But, startlingly, Leibo's putt didn't drop. The whole match depended on mine.

"Back of the hole, pro," said Delroy. "Don't be short."

If I'd learned anything about my golf game during the past eighteen months it was this: The longer I stare at the ball, the more likely I am to botch the shot.

So I made a brisk and radical decision to take my brain out of the process—a strategy that I highly recommend. With uncharacteristic resolve and no cognitive activity whatsoever, I stepped up to the putt and sank it for the win.

Leibo was ecstatic. "How's the old sphincter now, partner?" he crowed.

Delroy chucked me on the shoulder. "Good putt, mon. **Good** putt."

Winning felt terrific, but I knew it was a high that couldn't last. What I didn't know was how low I could go in the other direction.

Our final match of the day was set on Quail Valley's devious back nine, and pitted us against two more guys (call them Rob and Roger) who were impossible not to like. On the second hole I pounded a big drive and—avoiding the 56 degree wedge as if it were a hot poker—I stubbed what was meant to be a cute 7-iron punch. Quite by mistake, the shot morphed into a bumpy eighty-yard putt that died pin-high. From there I made par and we won the hole.

The Downhill Lie

Early on, our team was looking strong. Leibo and I covered efficiently for each other; even when we both stumbled, we scored. Both of us three-putted for bogeys on the par-5 14th, yet we still won it. Heading into the tough final stretch, we led by 3½ points and, for the first time all day, we felt in control.

The most humbling stretch of the course is the last four holes, and I was getting a stroke on each of them. Translation: Choke-mania.

I three-putted No. 15, which cost us a point. On No. 17 Leibo's tee shot veered into the lake, so it was up to me to carry the load—and I blew that hole, too.

Meanwhile Roger had gotten downright deadly on the greens. He was using a Viagra-blue ball and putting sidesaddle, a style popularized by Sam Snead in his later years. It worked rather well. Approaching the last tee, he and Rob now were only one down.

Both struck nice drives, as did Leibo and I. It was my second shot that was extraordinarily vile, an ankle-high screamer that slammed into the second of three bunkers below the elevated green. With no trouble at all, I blasted my ball into one of the other traps, and from there flung it cleanly over the putting surface.

Leibo's third shot, a short lob, dropped sweetly on the front edge, bit for one teasing nanosecond, then rolled all the way back down the hill and stopped near his feet. He shook his head, pitched up again and nearly holed it for a par.

With the pin location on the first tier, my only chance of saving victory was a sixty-foot downhill chip from the rough above the upper level. As far as I know, that ball is still rolling.

Roger, who was also stroking, canned his par putt and won the hole for his team. The match ended in a 5–5 tie, which stung as badly as a defeat. "We dropped 3½ points in four holes," Leibo noted glumly. "That's not too good."

The Downhill Lie

He was more annoyed with himself than with me, but he was also too classy to state the obvious: I flopped when he needed me to hang tough. I was, in fact, baggage.

Mercifully, there was no documentation of individual scores. Because of the best-ball format, one (and sometimes both) of us picked up if the hole was settled before we could putt out. The way I'd collapsed in that third match, I'd have been lucky to break 50.

It was withering to recall that only six months earlier I'd played those same nine holes at 4-over-par—whatever happened to that guy? Where the hell did he go?

"We'll get 'em tomorrow, doctor," Delroy said with a consoling nod, and lugged away our bags.

Later, beers in hand, Leibo and I approached the scoreboard to assess the damage. As incredible as it seemed, we were only three points behind the leaders in our flight.

"A miracle," Leibo murmured. "We actually have a chance."

Even after walking twenty-seven holes, I

wasn't as tired as I'd hoped to be. Sleep came fitfully, once again with visions of sh____.

The next morning, we arrived at Quail Valley early. To get the mojo juices flowing, I purchased a new hat and a new glove. The Mind Drive capsules had been a total bust, but I swallowed another one in the hope that an accrued dosage might work better.

Two nine-hole matches remained, and the opener began on No. 9, a dogleg par-4 that in previous rounds had given Leibo fits. Our opponents were a father-son team that was doing well in our flight. Senior was a sharp putter; Junior was raw power.

It was another magnificent day, clear and calm, the fairways shimmering with dew. We had the honors and, knowing I was a basket case, Leibo told me to go first. He said it would be good for my confidence. I considered teeing up with my left hand, as the Leadbetter coach had suggested, but my fingers were too shaky; both mitts were required to erect the ball properly.

The hole starts uphill, banks downward to

the left and then rises again to a knoll where the slender green is situated. I purposely set up off center, aiming to shave the corner, clear the crest and get a friendly roll on the downslope. Stunningly, that's what happened. I hammered the piss out of the ball, leaving myself 108 yards to the flag. The tee shot is worth recounting only because it proved to be the highlight of my whole match, and I squandered it.

What followed was a skulled punch, a bladed pitch, two flails in a bunker and a sheepish pickup. Leibo barely missed a six-footer for par, and already we were down a point.

On the following hole I made six-for-five, which helped us not at all. Next came a par-3 that I'd been playing well—and sure enough, I landed a 5-iron inside of Junior's ball. Because I was getting a handicap stroke, a two-putt would have won the point for us.

The green was devilishly fast, and I was facing a twenty-footer. "Just tap it," Delroy said, and I took the advice literally.

The ball rolled perhaps six feet. Under more casual circumstances it might have been humorous, but not at that moment. I ended up three-putting, so we halved the hole.

From then on it was a nonstop bloodbath. My next four tee shots were, in order: dunked, topped, sliced out of bounds and beached on the bank of a drainage ditch. Mojo-wise, the new hat was worthless; even Dad's gold watch couldn't spark a rally.

Before long, my role in the match diminished to that of a ghost. Senior and Junior forgot about me, and concentrated exclusively on beating Leibo. Occasionally Delroy would have to remind them, for their own safety, that I was still walking the course.

On the next-to-last hole, the 520-yard par-5, I recovered from a poor drive with two good shots in a row—a veritable hot streak. Leibo and I were both eying birdie attempts in the fifteen-foot range, and feeling better. That's when Junior pitched in for an eagle from thirty yards.

The Downhill Lie

Delroy turned to me and shrugged. "It's just not your day, captain."

With one hole remaining, we were now down by 3 and playing for pride. After Junior pushed his tee shot into the water, his father loudly topped one that sputtered 175 yards on a surreal, flawless vector, straight to the green.

"You'll have to teach me that one," Leibo said, stepping to the tee. Despite a vicious crosswind off the lake, he fired a laser twelve feet from the pin.

I followed with a towering 4-iron that caught a thermal and drifted off line, plopping into the neck of a greenside bunker. Having failed to execute a proper sand shot all day, I amazed myself by floating it softly out of the trap; the ball hopped gently down the hill and rolled to within ten feet of the cup.

Said Leibo: "You actually looked like you knew what you were doing on that one."

Sinking that sucker would have been an inspiring finish, but it wasn't necessary. Leibo easily got his par, Senior three-putted and we took the hole—a puny morale booster after a doleful morning.

During our lunch break, Leibo scouted the leader board and reported that we'd fallen to last place in our flight. Although we weren't mathematically eliminated, the odds of rebounding to victory were slim. "We have a better chance of getting abducted by aliens," Leibo said.

The last match started on No. 16, the long downhill par-3. Our opponents were two brothers, say Mickey and Malcolm, neither of whom made the green. Nor did Leibo.

I struck another acceptable 4-iron but the wind strangled it. My ball stalled in the least desirable location of the putting surface, with no smooth line to the hole. To make the putt, I'd have to scoot it forty feet over a hump, across an intruding burr of fringe.

Delroy, who had remained upbeat in the face of almost-certain defeat, told me to pitch the ball. It was a shot I'd never before attempted, practiced or contemplated.

The Downhill Lie

Moreover, I'd recently watched Phil Mickelson, who owns one of the great short games of all time, try the same play and chunk a small crater in the green.

Without hesitation, I chickened out and reached for my putter. The result wasn't pretty; I might as well have used a shoe. I scrambled for a 4, which was as good as a par, and we halved the point. On No. 17, another stroking opportunity, I made a five-for-four to keep the match level.

Approaching the tee at No. 18—for me, the most ungovernable hole at Quail Valley—I vowed not to repeat the previous day's meltdown. Then, uncannily, I did just that.

The only difference in my hapless shot sequence was that this time I employed a fairway wood instead of a rescue club to locate the front bunkers. My subsequent moonshot over the green was a carbon of the one I'd launched in the third match.

Fleeting redemption occurred, under pressure, on the next par-5. Malcolm and I were both stroking, but his approach was dead on the stick, as usual. For a 14-handicapper, he was freakishly accurate with his long irons.

Fifty feet from the hole, I was praying just to park my lag somewhere in the same zip code. For once I thought my pace was perfect, yet the ball coasted four feet past the cup. Malcolm missed his bird but he was in with a five-for-four, which meant we'd lose the point if I didn't save my par.

"Left center," Delroy said. "Don't quit on it, pro."

Thunk. Back of the hole. I remember nothing but the sound of the ball landing in the cup; my brain was blissfully blank.

"Now **that,**" said Delroy, "was a putt."

Leibo gave a congratulatory knuckle-bump and said, "You saved us on that one."

A small luminous moment, in a day of many failures.

On No. 13, I went exploring. Instead of pulling my drive into a necklace of cruel fairway bunkers (my usual route to the flag), I sliced it completely out of sight. I told Leibo and the two brothers to play on ahead; I'd catch up later.

My ball had settled in a sandy knot of weeds near the edge of a citrus grove. I tried blasting a rescue club, and the shot dribbled all of forty yards.

For my next trick, I'd have to shoot the ball virtually straight up in order to clear a steep hill, the crown of which was adorned with young oaks. Even better, the angle was completely blind.

Delroy waved down and called out, "Aim here, between these trees!" Then he hastily ducked for cover.

This time the rescue club lived up to its name. I ran to the top of the hill in time to see my ball drop close to the green, behind a small mound. I wasn't out of the hole; not yet.

"Welcome back," said Leibo, when I caught up to the others. "We thought you got lost."

Because I couldn't clear the knoll any other

way, I was forced to reconcile with the Vokey wedge. It was the same simple pitch that I'd practiced maybe three hundred times on the range, with occasional competency; one of several rudimentary shots that had mysteriously vanished from my meager arsenal in the days before the tournament.

Dreading another sh_ _ _, I silently recited what Steve Archer had told me: Turn, don't slide, away from the ball. **Turn, don't slide.**

And I assume that's what I did, because the ball dropped thirty feet from the flag and stuck like a dart. Then, with uncommon deliberation, I gutted the putt for a bogey.

Leibo hooted. "We call that a Daniel Boone!"

"Why?" I asked.

"Because you were in the wilderness the whole time."

Ba-da-boom.

The sparkle of the moment dimmed when Mickey nailed his par, leaving Leibo with a dicey fifteen-footer to halve the hole.

No problem. With two to play, we were only one down.

The Downhill Lie

Nobody bungled the par-5 14th, so all four of us were looking at birdies. My putt was by far the longest, forty-five feet downhill, breaking three balls left to right.

Delroy told me to let it rip. "Your partner's in good shape, mon. Don't hold back."

My line turned out to be perfect, although the speed was a bit muscular. The ball struck the back rim of the cup and popped into the air like a piece of toast, leaving a sickening six-footer for par. "You got no luck today," Delroy sighed, "no luck at all."

Before my stomach had time to knot, Leibo calmly stepped up and stroked his ball. It rolled eighteen feet to the lip and hung there, Delroy shouting, "Let him in! Let him in!"

Thunk. The ball dropped, and the point was ours.

Leibo smiled. I sagged with relief. Delroy made a fist and gave us a nod.

With one hole remaining, the score stood even. We probably had no chance to win the tournament, but it would have been grand to take the last match.

The final battleground was No. 15, a 386-yard par-4 that plays uphill, and almost always into a bracing wind. Peppered with bunkers, the hole carries the number two handicap rating at Quail Valley, although many members believe it is the hardest of all. Frequently it's the cruelest.

Leibo split the fairway as usual. I opted for drama, rolling my hands and duck-hooking my drive into a waste bunker the size of Rhode Island. Leibo whispered, "Don't worry, nobody's reaching this green in two today."

Wrong.

Both Malcolm and Mickey hit epic drives, followed by epic second shots that put them nicely on the putting surface, within birdie range. It was deflating, but we didn't wilt.

That would come later.

I made a rare smooth swing in the gritty sand, and clobbered my rescue club about as far as I could into that whistling wind. The ball landed on the steep side of a depression, sixty yards from the stick. Leibo was much closer and contemplating a short lob—his specialty.

Instead of tempting fate with another wedge shot, I reached for the 7-iron. Some might call it cowardly; I prefer the word "resourceful." In any event, I punched the ball too cleanly. It rolled through the break and off the green, cozying in the kinky fringe. A save from there would have been difficult for a scratch player.

Like me, Malcolm was getting a stroke on the hole. It meant that Leibo needed to sink his pitch or at least drop it close enough for a tap-in, to put pressure on the other team.

What he did was something I'd never seen him do—raise up on the downswing, which caused him to squirt the ball into a bunker. The shot was painful to watch. It reminded me of me.

Leibo was seething at himself, but in truth the hole was mine to win or lose. A par by

Malcolm was as good as a birdie, so our only chance was for Malcolm to three-putt, and for me to sink my shot from the edge of the green.

Delroy read the line as straight, and if I'd stroked it that way I might have lucked out and hit the pin. But the slope was like frozen grease, and the ball got away from me. Malcolm two-putted with ease, and the match was over. We lost 6–4.

Back at the clubhouse, Delroy hopped off the cart and shook our hands. When I apologized for the way I'd chopped up the course, he smiled and said, "It wasn't your week, that's all. That's golf, captain."

The next day, he would be flying to Jamaica to watch the world cricket championships. It sounded like a great way to forget about the tournament.

Leibo dragged me to the scoreboard for the postmortem. We finished with 21.5 points—not the worst of the forty-eight scores, by far, but low enough to dock us dead last in our flight.

I asked him, "When's the last time you finished last in one of these things?"

"Never," he replied. "But I feel good about it."

At first I figured he was being a smartass, but he wasn't. "Are you kidding?" he said. "Three days of beautiful weather on a beautiful golf course—what's better than that?"

How about a partner who doesn't fold like a cheap accordion?

"Lighten up, would you? It was your first tournament," Leibo said. "I'll be very disappointed if you don't ask me back next year."

"That may be the next time I play golf," I said.

"Seriously. I had fun."

"But you carried me the whole way! I was useless."

"That's not true," Leibo insisted. "You had a couple of bad nines, that's all."

Which is like saying: Don't let an iceberg or two spoil the whole cruise.

After a snack, we grabbed a cart and rode

out to watch the playoff among the eight pairs that had won their flights. The format required teammates to take alternating shots, with scoring adjusted for the differing handicaps.

The scene reminded me of a Mad Max movie—sixteen harried golfers pursued by a streaming convoy of Club Cars, many of the riders enjoying adult beverages. I couldn't imagine trying to steady myself over a golf ball amid a throng like that; the possibilities for soul-scarring indignity seemed boundless.

Later, Leibo returned some business calls while I pensively assessed the tournament experience. Playing forty-five competitive holes against ten strangers was no light-hearted romp for a reclusive, neurotic, doubt-plagued duffer. To sink that clinching putt in our only victory was a gas, but overall my performance had been sloppy and unpoised. Worse, I'd let down my partner and friend, who was too kind to say so.

Before leaving Quail Valley, I tossed the blister pack of Mind Drive capsules into a garbage can. Eventually I'd have lost the damn things, anyway.

Day 577

The day after the tournament ends, I drive out to Quail Valley resolved not to swing a club—and I don't.

Because I'm burned out. Fried. Whipped.

For a year and a half, I worked hard, played adequately in spurts, and now I've smacked the wall and spun out.

Facts are facts: I am not a young man with untapped talents, supple joints and nerves of titanium (or even Titallium, whatever that is). Tomorrow I'll be fifty-four years old, and the limits to what I can achieve on a golf course have been starkly presented. A strong case could be made that I should park my sticks for another thirty years.

But today is a dazzling March morning,

breezy and cloudless, and despite the fresh wounds from the tournament it feels all right to be standing in the sun on the practice range, just watching.

The mighty Quinn wields a midget driver, while his beautiful mother is trying out a new 5-wood. They're both spanking the ball, and they're happy. When the sport is new, every crisp shot is a wonder and a thrill.

I believe this is how you're supposed to feel with a golf club in your hands: Full of heart and free of mind. This is the whole slippery secret; the only way to survive, and possibly enjoy, the game. Hit the ball, forget about it, then hit the ball again.

Quinn's current swing model is part Tiger Woods, part Russell Crowe with a barstool. With a grunt he tops the shot and finishes in a comic pretzel, holding the pose.

From under his crooked visor he peers at me with a sheepish expression. "I looked up, didn't I?"

The Downhill Lie

"Don't worry about it."

He tees up another one and bangs it a hundred yards straight down the pipe. He spins around, grinning proudly, to make sure I saw the shot.

For a second, I'm a kid again and my father is standing behind me on the range, watching me whack one ball after another. And I can recall exactly how fantastic it felt to pound one—really crush it—then peek back to catch the look on Dad's face.

I'm wondering if he knew what those Sundays meant to me; if he understood that even when I was playing poorly and fuming like a brat, there was nowhere else I'd rather have been, and no one else I'd rather have been with. I hope I told him so, but, sadly, I cannot remember.

Now Quinn Hiaasen, who never got to meet his grandfather or see him hit a golf ball, says, as if on cue: "Dad, this is so much fun!"

Word for word, I swear to God.

The Sweet Spot

When my mother asked how the tournament went, I answered with glum honesty: "Not too well. On some holes it was horrible, like I'd never touched a club before."

I didn't mention that I'd worn Dad's watch for good luck. No mojo was potent enough to have saved me from myself.

"Was it your putting?" she asked delicately.

"A little bit of everything, Mom."

"But wasn't this the first golf tournament you've ever been in?"

"Yup," I said, "and very possibly the last."

"So you didn't have fun?"

Again with the fun.

"That's a good question," I said.

Since it was Mom on the other end, there was no choice but to tell the truth. "Some of it was fun," I conceded.

The Downhill Lie

She understood completely. Golf is a vexing, soul-stomping sport for perfectionists, and she'd been married to one.

I recall often hearing my father grumble after striking what appeared to me as a dandy shot. What I hadn't realized was that he'd hit an unintended fade instead of a draw, or that he'd been aiming left of the flag instead of right, or that he'd been trying to spin the ball dead at the front of the green instead of rolling it to the back. The shots that he'd executed so dependably in his twenties no longer flew easily and true, and Dad realized that his skills were slipping. I remember how quiet and weary-looking he became as his shoulder pain worsened and his scores began drifting into the mid- and then upper 80s, never to descend.

It's probably a blessing that I wasn't a low handicapper the first time around, when I was young, because otherwise the failure to play well in midlife would be withering and possibly unbearable. With mediocrity as my only personal frame of experience, I have no conception of how it must feel for a really good golfer to hit a really bad golf shot.

I do, however, know how it feels for a hacker to hit a good one. It feels great.

That's the killer. A good shot is a total rush, possibly the second most pleasurable sensation in the human experience. It will mess with your head in wild and delusive ways.

One day I took Mike Lupica to play Quail Valley. The course was gusty and heartless, typical for early spring. After parring the first two holes I commenced the Big Stumble, finishing with a 97 that included four ignominious putts on No. 16.

Lupica himself got mugged by the back nine, and slouched off muttering unprintable slurs about Messrs. Fazio and Price, the course designers.

Later, in a more reflective mood, he said: "You couldn't have picked a harder place to try to get good at golf. You have to factor that in when you're evaluating yourself—this course is really tough. . . . You're a good person trapped in an abusive relationship."

Here's what feeds the addiction: On No. 8, the most pitiless of the par-3s, I'd slashed a 4-iron through a savage crosswind, landing the ball six feet from the flag—one of those startling golden scenes that seem surreal at the moment.

That night, instead of sensibly fixating on the grisly four-putt at the 16th, I found myself reliving that lovely tee shot on the 8th as if it wasn't the fluke that it was, but rather a lightning glimpse of my true potential. Hope bloomed like a staph infection, and I was back at Quail Valley the very next day.

The Member-Guest had provided so few such moments that rosy self-deception was impossible. Leibo kept urging me to focus on the good holes, but the highlight reel was woefully brief.

There was The Putt, that tricky three-footer that I'd sunk for our one and only win. As thrilling as that dinky little par had been at the time, alone it seemed hardly enough to justify prolonging a struggle that had taken a melancholy turn.

An impartial review of scores from the past nineteen months would confirm that I'd peaked the previous autumn, and was now skidding downhill toward an unacceptably ragged level of play.

Maybe the time had come to quit all over again, while the brighter memories remained vivid and untainted. . . .

That eagle with a 9-iron from the fairway bunker on No. 7.

Those three birdies I'd made one morning with Bill Becker.

The absurdly long, sidehill sand shot that I'd nearly holed out with Lupica last summer at Noyac.

A 306-yard drive that I'd hit with Leibo, chortling, during the practice round of the tournament.

And that singular shining round of 85, which seemed destined to stand forever as my personal best.

The comeback had unfolded as neither a

storybook tale nor a total fiasco. I'd reached my two simple goals of besting the lowest eighteen-hole score of my youth, and of completing a tournament without crumbling to pieces.

What I had **not** been able to do was to get good enough at golf to be satisfied. Such a distant state of mind might be attainable, but slogging onward carries the risk of poisoning me forever against the game, which would be a damn shame.

The decision won't be easy. As every golf addict knows, all it takes is one great shot to keep you hooked.

Sometimes it doesn't even have to be your own.

D-Day

In the weeks following the tournament, I've played a couple of rounds without disaster or distinction. The orthopedic surgeon says there's not much to be done about my bum knee, and advises me to take a pill whenever it hurts.

On the day after tomorrow I'm supposed to show up at the PGA complex in Port St. Lucie as a one-day substitute in an informal tournament that includes a half-dozen of my old high school classmates. I'm reluctant to put my present golf game on display, but it's a favor for Leibo—the least I can do after conscripting him for my Member-Guest. After this I'll be able to throw out my Callaways and have a clear conscience.

Or not.

From Feherty comes droll Irish advice: "Finish the book, and **then** give up golf again. That way you'd feel good twice in the same day."

Not a bad plan, although it's possible that he's kidding.

This afternoon I drive Quinn out to the Sandridge Golf Club, where I haven't shown my face since sinking that cart. I wear no disguise, but I tiptoe past the pro shop like it's Ann Coulter's sex dungeon.

The club hosts a weekly clinic for

youngsters, and today's event is a three-hole "scramble." First prize: An honor pin from the Disney Wildlife Conservation Fund, which has nothing to do with golf but it looks pretty cool.

Since I haven't a clue how a scramble works, Quinn's coach patiently explains: The kids are paired in teams and play off the best ball. Each golfer takes a shot from that lie, the best ball is again chosen, and on it goes.

Quinn's partner is a tall, sturdy kid named Dakota, who is blessed with a splendid short game. Quinn's having a banner day with his driver ("The Big Boy," he calls it), so the two of them are ham-and-egging from tee to green. My job is to pilot the cart and, still skittish from my last tour of The Lakes, I navigate with heightened caution.

Approaching the final hole, a par-3, we think that our team might be leading the match. Quinn belts another straight drive,

Dakota pitches to the fringe and moments later we're putting for bogey.

Both boys are a bit exuberant with their lags, and now there's a ten-footer sneering back at us. Dakota goes first, the ball dying two inches shy of the lip.

The other players, who finished a few minutes ahead of our team, are gathered at greenside with their parents and the coach. Except for a couple of kids playing tag around the bunkers, everybody watches quietly as Quinn Hiaasen lines up his putt.

"Just take your time," is Dad's brilliant contribution to the effort.

Showing no fear, no yips and—most importantly—no genetic predisposition to choke, my youngest son drills the ball straight into the back of the hole. I am totally surprised. Quinn is not.

The small crowd breaks into applause— Quinn and his buddy have won by 4 strokes. The coach presents the medals, and gently cautions against overcelebrating. There will be days, she says, when it's someone else's turn to win, and your turn to clap.

Back in the cart, my boy is chattering and antic with joy. The great part is, he'd be no different if he had missed the putt. Sometimes it's astonishing to think we have the same DNA.

When I put him on the phone with his mother, Quinn adopts a more Norwegian attitude about his first golfing victory. "It's just a kids' tournament, Mom," he says.

Nice try, but I couldn't help notice the 500-watt smile when his ball dropped in the cup; the glow was unforgettable. There's nothing to do but admit the truth: Regardless of my own foolish and overwrought tribulations, this really is a great game. Truly it is.

I see warmer days ahead, when a certain young player might want his old man to join him for nine holes after school. For some reason he enjoys watching me hit the ball, so I suppose I'll bring my clubs.

What the hell.

A NOTE ABOUT THE AUTHOR

Carl Hiaasen was born and raised in Florida. He is the author of fourteen novels and two children's books. He also writes a weekly column for **The Miami Herald**.

LIKE WHAT YOU'VE SEEN?

If you enjoyed this large print edition of
THE DOWNHILL LIE, here is another book
by Carl Hiaasen also available in large print.

NATURE GIRL
(hardcover)
978-0-7393-2626-8 • 0-7393-2626-0
$28.95/$38.95C

Large print books are available wherever books
are sold and at many local libraries.

All prices are subject to change. Check with your
local retailer for current pricing and availability.
For more information on this and other large print titles,
visit www.randomhouse.com/largeprint.